DARTMOOR

Pathfinder® Guides

Short Walks

Compiled by
Sue Viccars

Dedication
For my sons Nick and Joffy.

Acknowledgements
Special thanks are due to Dr Tom Greeves for kindly casting his expert eye over my original manuscript, and for fine-tuning historical details.

Text:	Sue Viccars
Photography:	Sue Viccars
Editorial:	Ark Creative (UK) Ltd
Design:	Ark Creative (UK) Ltd

ISBN 978-0-319-09017-6

First published 2002 by Jarrold Publishing. Revised and reprinted in 2005.

This edition first published in Great Britain 2009 by Crimson Publishing and reprinted with amendments in 2013, 2016 and 2017.

Crimson Publishing, 19-21C Charles Street, Bath, BA1 1HX

www.pathfinderwalks.co.uk

Printed in India by Replika Press Pvt. Ltd. 7/17

A catalogue record for this book is available from the British Library.

Front cover: Chagford
Previous page: River Plym below Cadover Bridge

Contents

	Keymap	4
	At-a-glance	6
	Introduction	11
Short walks up to 3½ miles		
1	*Birch Tor and Vitifer Mines*	16
2	*Chagford and the River Teign*	20
3	*Haytor Quarry and Tramway*	24
4	*Hound Tor and Hayne Down*	28
5	*Lydford*	32
6	*North and South Brentor*	36
7	*The Teign Gorge at Castle Drogo*	40
8	*Trenchford and Tottiford Reservoirs*	44
Slightly longer walks of 3½ to 4½ miles		
9	*Avon Dam and Rider's Rings*	48
10	*Bonehill Rocks*	52
11	*Crazywell Pool*	56
12	*The East and West Okement Rivers*	60
13	*Foggintor and Swelltor Quarries*	65
14	*Scorhill*	69
15	*The Dewerstone*	74
16	*Wistman's Wood*	78
Longer walks of 5 miles or more		
17	*Dr Blackall's Drive*	83
18	*Fernworthy and Grey Wethers*	88
19	*Harford and the Erme Valley*	93
20	*Meldon Reservoir and Blackator Copse*	98
	Further Information	103
	Answers to Questions	109

Keymap

SCALE 1:277 777 or 1 INCH to about 4½ MILES *1CM to 2.7KM*

0 2 4 6 8 10 KILOMETRES 15

0 2 4 6 MILES 8 10

KEYMAP HEIGHTS SHOWN IN METRES

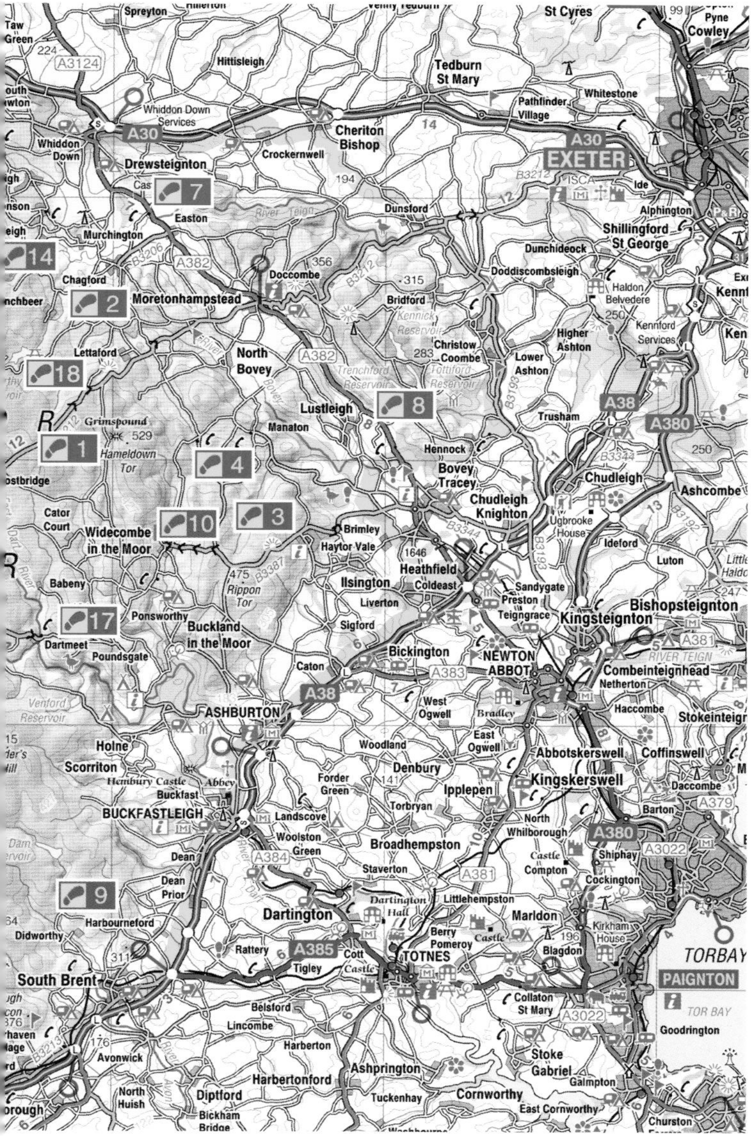
Spreyton
Taw Green
224
A3124
Hittisleigh
Tedburn St Mary
St Cyres
Pyne
Cowley
Whiddon Down Services
A30
Whiddon Down
Cheriton Bishop
Pathfinder Village
Whitestone
14
Crockernwell
Drewsteignton
A30
EXETER
7
194
B3212
ISCA
Ide
River Teign
Easton
Dunsford
12
Alphington
Murchington
Shillingford St George
14
B3206
A382
356
Dunchideock
Chagford
Doccombe
Doddiscombsleigh
2
Moretonhampstead
B3212
315
Haldon Belvedere
Bridford
250
Kennick Reservoir
Kennford Services
Lettaford
North Bovey
A382
Higher Ashton
283
Christow
Coombe
Lower Ashton
18
Trenchford Reservoir
Tottiford Reservoir
B3193
8
A38
Lustleigh
Trusham
A380
Grimspound
529
Manaton
1
Hameldown Tor
Hennock
250
4
Bovey Tracey
B3344
Chudleigh
Postbridge
Ashcombe
Chudleigh Knighton
13
Cator Court
10
3
Brimley
Ugbrooke House
B3192
Widecombe in the Moor
Haytor Vale
B3344
1646
Ideford
Luton
475
B3387
Heathfield
B3193
Babeny
Rippon Tor
Ilsington
Coldeast
Sandygate
Preston
Liverton
Bishopsteignton
17
Ponsworthy
Teigngrace
Kingsteignton
Buckland in the Moor
Sigford
5
A381
Dartmeet
Poundsgate
6
Bickington
NEWTON ABBOT
River Teign
Combeinteignhead
Caton
A383
Netherton
A38
7
West Ogwell
Haccombe
Venford Reservoir
ASHBURTON
Bradley
Stokeinteignhead
East Ogwell
Holne
Woodland
Abbotskerswell
Coffinswell
Scorriton
Denbury
Hembury Castle
Abbey
Forder Green
141
Ipplepen
Kingskerswell
Daccombe
Buckfast
A379
BUCKFASTLEIGH
Torbryan
North Whilborough
Barton
Landscove
10
Woolston Green
Broadhempston
A380
Dean
A384
Castle Compton
Shiphay
A3022
Staverton
A381
Cockington
8
Dean Prior
9
Dartington Hall
Littlehempston
Dartington
Marldon
Harbourneford
Berry Pomeroy
Castle
196
Kirkham House
Didworthy
Rattery
A385
Cott
TOTNES
Blagdon
TORBAY
311
6
Tigley
Castle
5
PAIGNTON
South Brent
Collaton St Mary
TOR BAY
Belsford
A3022
6
Goodrington
Lincombe
176
Harberton
B3213
Avonwick
Stoke Gabriel
Ashprington
Galmpton
Harbertonford
North Huish
Diptford
Tuckenhay
Cornworthy
Bickham Bridge
East Cornworthy
Churston

At-a-glance

1

Birch Tor and Vitifer Mines

- Tin mine remains
- heather moors
- Bronze Age site
- wonderful views

Walk Distance
$1\frac{3}{4}$ miles (2.8km)
Time
1 hour
Refreshments
Warren House Inn just south west of the car park

Narrow moorland path to Birch Tor; short clamber out of heathery gully towards end of walk

p. 16

Walk Completed

2

Chagford and the River Teign

- Stannary town
- stone bridges
- meadows
- waterside path

Walk Distance
2 miles (3.2km)
Time
1 hour
Refreshments
Several pubs and cafés in Chagford; try the excellent New Forge on the square

Level field and riverside paths; quiet lanes

p. 20

Walk Completed

3

Haytor Quarry and Tramway

- Deserted quarry
- granite tramway
- craggy tors
- moorland views

Walk Distance
$1\frac{1}{2}$ miles (2.4km)
Time
1 hour
Refreshments
Ice cream van in car park; the Rock Inn at Haytor Vale just to the east

Level grassy former tramway

p. 24

Walk Completed

4

Hound Tor and Hayne Down

- Granite tors
- Jay's Grave
- Bowerman's Nose
- medieval village

Walk Distance
$3\frac{1}{2}$ miles (5.6km)
Time
2 hours
Refreshments
Refreshments van Easter–end September, and winter holidays and weekends

Uneven rocky path from Hayne Down to Hayne; steep climb up the lane from Great Houndtor Farm to the cattle-grid

p. 28

Walk Completed

5

Lydford

- Medieval 'castle'
- Lych Way
- moorland views
- St Petrock's Church

Walk Distance
$2\frac{1}{4}$ miles (3.6km)

Time
1 hour

Refreshments
The Castle Inn and Hotel, Lydford; Dartmoor Inn at the Lydford turning on the A386

Quiet lanes and tracks; gradual ascent onto moorland edge

p.32

Walk Completed ☐

6

North and South Brentor

- Old railway
- moorland views
- rolling farmland
- Brent Tor church

Walk Distance
3 miles (4.8km) + $1\frac{1}{2}$ mile (2.4km) possible extension

Time
$1\frac{1}{2}$ hours (+1 hr)

Refreshments
None en route; the Castle Inn at Lydford

Rocky uneven descent to Wortha Mill; steep climb up to church (optional)

p. 36

Walk Completed ☐

7

The Teign Gorge at Castle Drogo

- Wooded gorge
- hill forts
- castle & gardens
- craggy tors

Walk Distance
$2\frac{1}{2}$ miles (4km)

Time
$1\frac{1}{4}$ hours

Refreshments
National Trust shop and café at the castle; Sandy Park Inn

Good level path along top of gorge; dogs are not allowed into Castle Drogo and gardens

p. 40

Walk Completed ☐

8

Trenchford and Tottiford Reservoirs

- Forest walks
- picnic sites
- rhododendrons
- lakeside birdlife

Walk Distance
$2\frac{1}{2}$ miles (4km)

Time
$1\frac{1}{4}$ hours

Refreshments
None en route. Cleave public house in Lustleigh

Woodland paths around reservoirs; no real ascents or descents. *Note that dogs should be kept on leads*

p. 44

Walk Completed ☐

At-a-glance

Slightly longer walks of 3½ to 4½ miles

9	10	11	12

Avon Dam and Rider's Rings	*Bonehill Rocks*	*Crazywell Pool*	*The East and West Okement Rivers*
• Waterfalls • superb scenery • Bronze Age site • huge dam	• Dramatic tors • Widecombe • moorland views • pretty inns	• Moorland pool • forest paths • Devonport Leat • aqueduct	• Castle • beech woods • stepping stones • waterfalls
Walk Distance 4 miles (6.4km) **Time** 2 hours **Refreshments** None en route; picnic tables near Long-a-traw; range of pubs and cafés in South Brent	**Walk Distance** 3½ miles (5.6km) + 1¾ mile (3.8km) possible extension **Time** 1¾ hours (+1 hr) **Refreshments** Pubs & cafés in Widecombe	**Walk Distance** 3½ miles (5.6km) **Time** 2 hours **Refreshments** None en route; Royal Oak pub at Meavy south west of Burrator Reservoir	**Walk Distance** 4½ miles (7.2km) **Time** 2¾ hours **Refreshments** Good range of pubs and cafés in Okehampton
Tarmac lane then indistinct and rough walk across open moorland from Avon Dam to Rider's Rings	Rocky paths between the tors; steep walk down and back through Bonehill (extension)	Woodland tracks, rough moorland; steep rocky downhill path to the River Meavy	Occasionally rocky and narrow path by East Okement river; short yet steep climb through Halstock Wood
p. 48	p. 52	p. 56	p. 60
Walk Completed ☐	Walk Completed ☐	Walk Completed ☐	Walk Completed ☐

13

Foggintor and Swelltor Quarries

- Moorland tracks
- tramways
- granite quarries
- archaeology

Walk Distance
3½ miles (5.6km)

Time
1½ hours

Refreshments
None en route; pubs and cafés in Princetown; also the Dartmoor Inn at Merrivale

Brief rocky scramble around the edge of a gully at Swelltor Quarry

p.65

Walk Completed ☐

14

Scorhill

- Stone circle
- clapper bridges
- Kes Tor
- castle ruin

Walk Distance
4½ miles (7.2km)

Time
2¼ hours

Refreshments
None en route; Northmore Arms at Wonson; several pubs and cafés in Chagford

Rough moorland for first half of walk; steep woodland path down to River Teign and back up through Gidleigh Woods

p. 69

Walk Completed ☐

15

The Dewerstone

- Granite crags
- stone bridges
- wooded valley
- good views

Walk Distance
3¾ miles (6km)

Time
2 hours

Refreshments
Ice cream van in car parks; Royal Oak pub in Meavy; White Thorn Inn in Shaugh Prior

Steep, rocky descent towards Dewerstone Crags; uneven, narrow path through North Wood

p. 74

Walk Completed ☐

16

Wistman's Wood

- Ancient woodland
- stepping stones
- Devonport Leat
- moorland views

Walk Distance
4½ miles (7.2km)

Time
2½ hours

Refreshments
Pubs and cafés in Princetown; cream teas in summer at Powder Mills

Rough, open moorland beyond Wistman's Wood; river crossing at weir or on granite boulders

Do not attempt this walk after very heavy rainfall!

p. 78

Walk Completed ☐

At-a-glance

17	18	19	20

Dr Blackall's Drive	*Fernworthy and Grey Wethers*	*Harford and the Erme Valley*	*Meldon Reservoir and Blackator Copse*
• Granite tors • wooded valleys • ford • scenic drive	• Stone circles • remote moorland • forest track • tranquil reservoir	• Waterfalls • a Brunel viaduct • wooded valley • pretty hamlet	• Highest tors • nature reserves • ancient oak wood • moorland streams
Walk Distance 5¼ miles (8.4km) **Time** 2½ hours **Refreshments** None en route; mobile refreshments in the car park at times	**Walk Distance** 5½ miles (8.4km) **Time** 2½ hours **Refreshments** Mobile café sometimes in car park; good range of pubs and cafés in Chagford	**Walk Distance** 5 miles (8km) **Time** 2½ hours **Refreshments** None en route; picnic tables by the Erme; pubs and cafés in Ivybridge	**Walk Distance** 5 miles (8km) **Time** 2½ hours **Refreshments** None en route; range of pubs and cafés in Okehampton
Steep ascent up the lane from the River Dart and through Park Wood; also up the lane from Lower Town to Leusdon church	Rough indistinct track across open moor from forest edge to Grey Wethers; dogs to be kept under close control around the reservoir (breeding birds)	Riverside path wet and rocky in places; steep ascent up lane from railway viaduct to Pithill Farm	Rough approach over moor to Black Tor; rocky path through Blackator Copse
p. 83	p. 88	p. 93	p. 98
Walk Completed ☐	Walk Completed ☐	Walk Completed ☐	Walk Completed ☐

Introduction

Dartmoor, the largest area of wild country in southern Britain, is somewhere that gets under the skin. Those who move to the area from elsewhere in the country either love it or loathe it; those born there may go away for a while, but tend to gravitate back sooner or later. Thousands of people simply miss Dartmoor altogether as they race through Devon each summer on the main roads around the north and south of the moor en route for a Cornish holiday. But from both the A38 in the south, and the A30 that skirts the northern edge of Dartmoor, you can get a tantalising glimpse of what lies beyond these tourist routes in the form of great swells of open moorland beyond South Brent and south of Okehampton. The eastern approach to the moor, along the B3212 via the undulating hills and wooded river valleys west of Exeter, is quite different, and brings with it a wonderful sense of anticipation as the moorland landscape unfolds beyond Moretonhampstead.

A varied landscape

Dartmoor is part of a vast, raised granite plateau, rising to 2,037ft (621m) at its highest point, High Willhays, that stretches for many miles to the west, emerging again at Bodmin Moor and West Penwith in Cornwall, and then the Isles of Scilly, lying 28 miles (45km) west-south-west of Land's End. The moor receives the full force of the prevailing south-westerly winds, and has a high annual rainfall; the most rain ever recorded was over 134 inches (342cm) in 1994 (though in an average year 80 inches [203cm] would be more usual). It can be a bleak and forbidding place in bad weather. Where the granite has been exposed to the elements frost, wind and rain have weathered it into fantastic blocks and shapes to form 'tors', the most famous and accessible of which is Haytor on the southern side of the moor. Further erosion of the granite blocks has resulted in clitter, small granite boulders, covering large areas on the slopes beneath the tors.

But Dartmoor is so much more than a wild moorland. The combination of high annual rainfall and unyielding granite has given rise to a number of beautiful rivers, most of which have their sources on the northern moor. Millions of years ago the granite plateau was tilted, so that the highest land now lies on the north and west of the moor, and most of the rivers flow south, emerging from areas of inhospitable bog to form small, sparkling moorland streams. Where they hit the softer shales, slates and limestone at the granite edge they have cut deep valleys, now thickly wooded – the Teign gorge at Castle Drogo, the Dart below Dr Blackall's Drive, the Avon and the Erme – which provide wonderful walking opportunities.

The human imprint

At first sight it is easy to believe that Dartmoor is a totally natural landscape, but nothing could be further from the truth. The moor has been settled since prehistoric times, and the wealth of Bronze Age remains, in the form of standing stones, stone circles and rows, enclosures and hut circles, is unrivalled elsewhere in the country. Dating from 2500BC to 750BC, about 5,000 hut circles have been identified, and it has been estimated that there could have been several thousand people living on the moor at that time in settlements such as that at Grimspound. Iron Age occupation is evident in the form of hillforts and earthworks, such as those near

The Rugglestone Inn, Widecome

the Dewerstone, and at Prestonbury Camp and Cranbrook Castle, overlooking the Teign gorge.

There has been plenty of industry, too: the moor has been mined for tin since medieval times, and evidence today is plentiful in the form of gullies and pits, and the ruins of huts and blowing houses, where tin was smelted. A system of leats (narrow channels carrying water) was created to improve water supplies to farms, mills and tin works, and latterly to supply the growing population of Plymouth. Many of these provide excellent routes for walkers today, as do the abandoned trackways associated with the disused granite quarries to be found near Princetown and Haytor. In more recent times, a number of reservoirs have been built around the fringes of the open moor, and these again offer great walking opportunities for those looking for a gentler route.

Dartmoor today

Dartmoor was given National Park status in 1951, and is managed by the Dartmoor National Park Authority. Operating from its headquarters at Parke in Bovey Tracey, the authority has the task of balancing the conflicting demands made on Dartmoor: those of agriculture, tourism, conservation, and the controversial use of part of the moor as a training ground for the army. Walkers should be aware of what purposes lie behind the creation of the National Parks: '...the conservation of the natural beauty, wildlife and cultural heritage of the area, and the promotion of the understanding and enjoyment of its special qualities by the public'.

In accordance with the wishes of the park authority, there is no doubt that the best way to explore Dartmoor is on foot. The walks in this book have all been devised to introduce the walker to a wide range of experiences, ranging from a gentle stroll through the forests around a moorland reservoir, to a tougher route across the open moor to explore the upper reaches of one of Dartmoor's loveliest rivers. The routes suggested avoid the 'honeypot' areas and concentrate instead on getting as far off the beaten track as possible, as quickly as possible, yet without tackling those vast, almost featureless expanses of high moorland where competent navigational skills are essential. Walks on moorland are often tougher underfoot than those in more 'civilised' countryside, and good walking boots are recommended, especially for the longer routes. As with any area of high ground, weather conditions can change rapidly, and the moor can be fog-bound even in mid-summer; for this reason only *Walks 2, 7* and *8* are suitable in all weathers.

With the introduction of '**gps enabled' walks**, you will see that this book now includes a list of waypoints alongside the description of the walk. We have included these so that you can enjoy the full benefits of GPS should you wish to. GPS is an amazingly useful and entertaining navigational aid, and you do not need to be computer literate to enjoy it.

GPS waypoint co-ordinates add value to your walk. You will now have the extra advantage of introducing 'direction' into your walking which will enhance your leisure walking and make it safer. Use of a GPS brings greater confidence and security and you will find you cover ground a lot faster should you need to.

For essential information on map reading and basic navigation, read the *Pathfinder Guide Map Reading Skills* by outdoor writer, Terry Marsh (ISBN 978-0-7117-4978-8). For more information on using your GPS, read the *Pathfinder Guide GPS for Walkers*, by GPS teacher and navigation trainer, Clive Thomas (ISBN 978-0-7117-4445-5). Both titles are available in bookshops or can be ordered online at www.pathfinderwalks.co.uk

Birch Tor and Vitifer Mines

- Tin-mining remains
- Bronze Age site
- heather moors
- wonderful views

walk 1

This easy yet fascinating walk skirts around the edge of one of the most significant areas of heather moorland on Dartmoor, much of it classified as a Site of Special Scientific Interest. It is prized not only for its wealth of rare lichens and birds, but also for the extensive and accessible evidence of the area's industrial heritage in the form of tin-mining gullies and workings.

The path to Grimspound

walk 1

START On the B3212 east of the Warren House Inn

DISTANCE $1\frac{3}{4}$ miles (2.8km)

TIME 1 hour

PARKING Bennett's Cross car park

ROUTE FEATURES Narrow moorland path to Birch Tor; short clamber out of heathery gully towards end of walk. *Keep a close eye on dogs and children during the closing stages of the walk.*

GPS WAYPOINTS
- (Start) SX 680 816
- A SX 680 817
- B SX 686 818
- C SX 689 810
- D SX 682 811

PUBLIC TRANSPORT Bus service from Exeter (via Moretonhampstead) and Plymouth

REFRESHMENTS Warren House Inn just south west of the car park

PUBLIC TOILETS None en route

PICNIC/PLAY AREA None

ORDNANCE SURVEY MAPS Explorer OL28 (Dartmoor), Landranger 191 (Okehampton & North Dartmoor)

Before you set out on this walk take a look at Bennett's Cross, just above the car park. This simple granite cross is named after a 16th-century miner. It is also on the line of the ancient track across the moor, followed today by the modern road, which dates from the late 18th century. Once at the cross, turn away from the road and walk towards the moor to meet a clear path (Two Moors Way) coming in from the right.

> Tin has been mined on Dartmoor since medieval times. **Vitifer, Birch Tor and Golden Dagger mines** were among the most important on Dartmoor, being worked extensively in the 19th and early 20th centuries. The last mine closed in 1930.

A Bear left and follow the path uphill. At the crest of the hill turn right **B** by a stone cairn and take the narrow path that winds through the heather to gain the farthest outcrop of Birch Tor, from which there are wonderful views of Grimspound and Hamel Down across the Challacombe Valley to the left, and over the mine workings at Vitifer to the right. Walk straight ahead from the tor and pick up a narrow path that bears left downhill; note a stone row on the hillside ahead. Meet a deep-cut stony path at a T-junction. (If you want to visit Grimspound, turn left here to pass Headland Warren Farm and gain the road, then turn right.)

Turn right **C** and pick your way along the rocky path, which becomes grassier as it drops down into the valley. This area is lovely all year round, with white hawthorn blossom in May and young bracken in June, gorse and heather in late summer, and bright red rowan berries in the autumn. At the valley bottom the path reaches a grassy track that runs along the valley from the Golden Dagger tin mine.

> * **Grimspound**, thought by many to be Dartmoor's finest prehistoric site, dates from around 1300BC. Situated below Hameldown Tor beside the Grimslake stream, it must have provided an attractive site, with good grazing, and was probably used for keeping stock safe. The remains of about two dozen hut circles have been found within the enclosure wall. The site's significance was fully realised through investigations by the Dartmoor Exploration Committee in 1894.

Turn right to pass a stream crossing left: a great picnic spot, with various granite ruins and enclosures. *Be aware, however, that some of the gullies and pits may be deep; keep an eye on your children.* If you want to go to the Warren House Inn at this point, turn left over the stream, then straight up the hill on an obvious track; this popular pub soon comes into view. Said to be the third-highest pub in England (but actually the tenth-highest) it sits at 1,400ft (427m) above sea level.

> ? *In what year was the fire – that has never been allowed to go out – in the Warren House Inn first established?*

To return to your car, go straight on, keeping the stream on the left. A few minutes later the path forks **D**; take the right path, and walk uphill (initially with a stream on the left), cross the stream, and keep uphill to pass an area of snaking willows on the right. The path levels off to enter a deep, flat-bottomed, grassy gully. Walk to the end of the gully

Bennett's Cross

Birch Tor

where you have to scramble up and out of it to the left; keep ahead through the heather to reach a narrow path at right angles. Turn right to return to the Bennett's Cross car park. ■

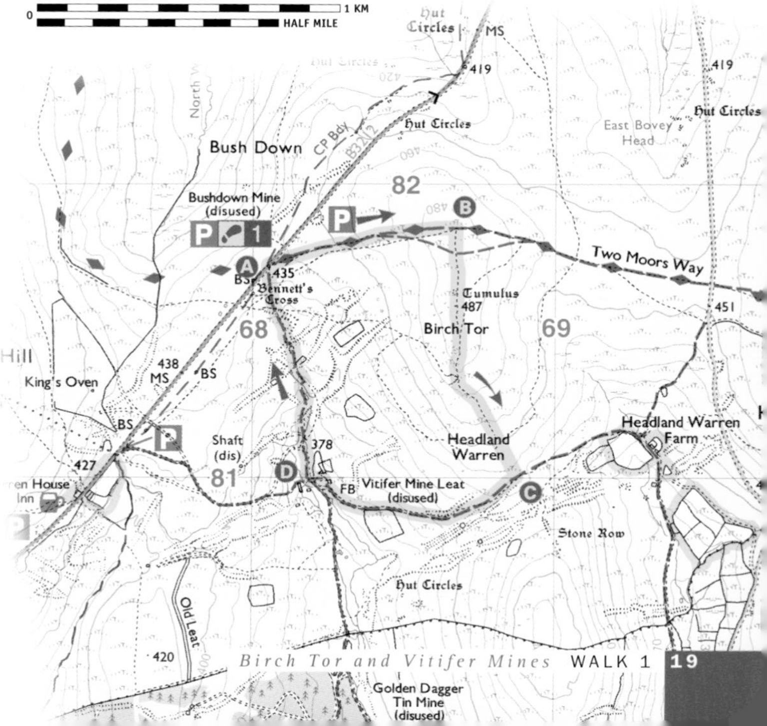

Chagford and the River Teign

- Old stannary town
- lovely meadows
- stone bridges
- waterside path

walk 2

Chagford is one of Dartmoor's most appealing small towns, nestling beneath lofty Meldon and Nattadon Commons on the north-eastern edge of the moor. With a fascinating history and a wealth of attractive buildings, this easy walk starts through its narrow, flower-filled streets to the lovely meadows along the River Teign, and back via the old market square and church.

The Pepper Pot, Chagford

walk 2

START Chagford

DISTANCE 2 miles (3.2km)

TIME 1 hour

PARKING Car park past the church (fee)

ROUTE FEATURES Level field and riverside paths; quiet lanes

GPS WAYPOINTS

- SX 702 874
- Ⓐ SX 701 875
- Ⓑ SX 694 880
- Ⓒ SX 699 881
- Ⓓ SX 705 882

PUBLIC TRANSPORT Bus service from Exeter and Okehampton

REFRESHMENTS Several pubs and cafés in Chagford; try the excellent New Forge on the square

PUBLIC TOILETS In the Pepper Pot in the square

PICNIC/PLAY AREA In Jubilee Park, by the car park

ORDNANCE SURVEY MAPS Explorer OL28 (Dartmoor), Landranger 191 (Okehampton & North Dartmoor)

* **Chagford** was confirmed by Edward I in 1305 as a stannary town where tin metal was brought for assaying and taxation, the whole process being known as the 'coinage' of tin. The other stannary towns in Devon were Tavistock, Ashburton and Plympton. At one time 40 per cent of Devon's tin production passed through Chagford, and it remained an important stannary town until the mid-17th century.

Leave the car park and turn left down the lane. Turn right down the High Street, past the Three Crowns Hotel on the left, said to be haunted by the ghost of Royalist Sidney Godolphin, who died of musket wounds here in 1643 during the Civil War.

Ⓐ Chagford was for many years an important market town. On reaching the square note the 'Pepper Pot', an octagonal market house, built in 1862 by Rev George Hayter Hames. Hames sponsored various town improvements, including a proper drainage system and water supply, and the installation of gas. In 1891 Chagford also became one of the first towns to enjoy water-powered electric street lighting. Continue straight on down Mill Street; at the fork keep right (Mill Street) downhill, signed Gidleigh and Throwleigh. At the bottom of the hill the lane bears right (Gidleigh Park Hotel straight on). The lane leads over one bridge, then crosses Chagford Bridge over the River Teign. There has been a bridge here since at least 1224, at the site of the ford that gave Chagford its name: 'chag' is dialect for gorse, hence 'Chagford'.

? *In the church there are a number of carved roof bosses. One shows three linked animals – can you see what they are?*

B Once over the bridge, turn right through a wooden gate on the Two Moors Way (no footpath sign). The path soon passes through a small wooden gate then continues along the riverside. Note the huge oak trees, which once grew out of a granite wall. Pass through a wooden gate at the field end, and continue to reach an open area where paddling is possible in the river. A converted mill lies on the opposite bank; with the demise of the tin industry, around 1700, Chagford played a significant role in the woollen industry, spinning wool for the prosperous weaving towns of East Devon. Later, around the mid-19th century, the town developed as a moorland holiday resort.

C Pass through a small, wooden gate and along the bottom of a large field, then over a wooden footbridge/gate, then another footbridge, then a gate, to enter mixed woodland by the weir. The path leaves the river to follow a leat (trench) on the right. Leave the woodland over a stile/gate, walk along the bottom of the next field, and through a wooden gate. At the end of the next field pass through a small wooden gate at a junction of paths; go straight on (signed Rushford Bridge). Walk through a strip of woodland, over a railed

* The **church of St Michael the Archangel** dates from the 15th century, but was much restored in the 19th century. Look for the inscription to Mary Whiddon on the sanctuary floor. The story goes that she was shot on the church steps immediately after her wedding on October 11, 1641; some say that R.D. Blackmore based part of his novel *Lorna Doone* on this tale.

footbridge to enter a field, then diagonally left through a gate in the hedge. Follow the path sign across the next field to join the lane via a gate.

D Turn right to cross Rushford Bridge; walk up the lane to meet the road. Turn right to pass the garage (left) and primary school (right). As you approach the square fork left at the bank, then under the archway into the churchyard. Head towards the west end of the church: if you want to have a look inside enter via the north door. Otherwise keep ahead round the west end, then bear right to leave the churchyard and reach the lane to the car park. ■

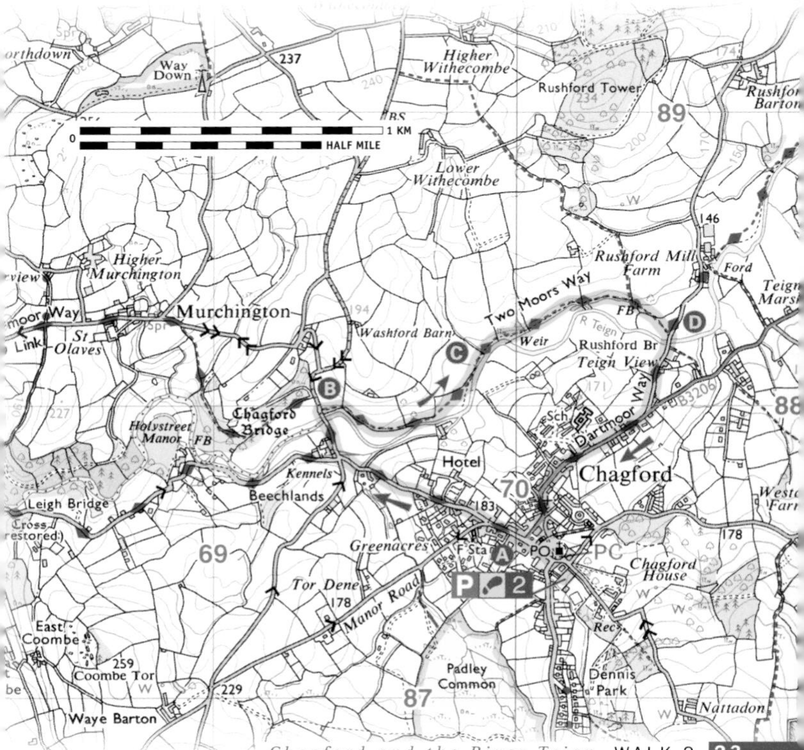

Haytor Quarry and Tramway

- Deserted quarry
- granite tramway
- craggy tors
- moorland views

walk 3

A gentle stroll across open moorland from the popular car park at Haytor leads to all kinds of surprises (and provides the opportunity to avoid the crowds ascending the slopes to Haytor Rocks). The route leads to the old Haytor Quarry before returning along the granite tramway, hinting that, historically, there is more to this part of the moor than meets the eye.

Haytor and the granite tramway

walk 3

START On the B3387 near Haytor

DISTANCE $1\frac{1}{2}$ miles (2.4km)

TIME 1 hour

PARKING In the lower Haytor car park (with National Park information centre)

ROUTE FEATURES Level grassy former tramway

GPS WAYPOINTS
- Start: SX 765 771
- A SX 761 775
- B SX 759 775
- C SX 758 778
- D SX 762 777

PUBLIC TRANSPORT Bus service from Newton Abbot, Buckfastleigh, Totnes, Tavistock, Okehampton

REFRESHMENTS Ice cream van in car park; the Rock Inn at Haytor Vale just to the east

PUBLIC TOILETS In car park

PICNIC/PLAY AREA None

ORDNANCE SURVEY MAPS Explorer OL28 (Dartmoor), Landranger 191 (Okehampton & North Dartmoor)

From the car park cross the road and walk straight ahead between two granite boulders on a broad, grassy path, running slightly uphill. Aim for the right side of the spoil heaps that can be seen ahead and keep going until you reach a flat, grassy area at the base of the highest heap; traces of the tramway can be seen on the level ground ahead right.

A Look to the left to find a deeply banked gully that leads into the quarry. Walk up the bank to the left of the gully, and then turn right through a small wooden gate in the wire fence. Once through the gate, follow the narrow path towards the first of two deep ponds. This is a great picnic spot, and wonderfully tranquil. Look around carefully and you will find all sorts of bolts and rings in the rocks, and some iron

> **Haytor Rocks** are the most popular, accessible and easily recognised of Dartmoor's tors. Those who would never dare to venture farther into the heart of the moor are happy to take the short walk up to the base of these spectacular rocks, rising 1,499ft (457m) above sea level. Their appeal as a tourist attraction first became apparent during the Victorian period. Fortunately, an early 20th-century scheme to construct a coal-fired electric tramway to improve access to the rocks came to naught.

winding gear still visible in the water: a reminder of the time around 100 men worked here. Quarrying began in 1820 under the ownership of George Templer (1781–1843) of Stover, when granite from Haytor was reputedly the cheapest on Dartmoor. The quarry was expanded in 1825 when it won the contract for supplying granite for work at the British Museum and for the arches of London Bridge. It fell largely into disuse around 1865 in the face of cheaper competition from Cornwall.

Tranquil waters in Haytor Quarry

Walk in a clockwise direction (left bank) around the two pools – look out for goldfish – to leave the quarry via a narrow, sandy path and stile **B** at the far end of the second pool. This emerges through a bank to join a grassy path; walk straight ahead to meet the granite tramway at right angles. George Templer built the tramway to transport granite eight miles (12.9km) to the head of the Stover Canal (built by his father, James, in 1792) at Teigngrace, from where it would be conveyed by barge to Teignmouth. By 1858 the tramway was disused.

> * The **granite tramway**, the first of its kind in Devon, was opened on September 16, 1820. Its design is simple; cheap, readily available granite was used to form flanged rails, along which teams of up to 18 horses pulled wooden-wheeled, open-sided, flat-bed carts. Fortunately, most of its route to the head of the Stover Canal runs slightly downhill.

C Turn right and follow the

granite tramway across the open moor, with stunning views to the left towards Greator Rocks and Hound Tor over the valley of the Becka Brook. The tramway curves right to reach a junction; turn right **D** and follow the 'branchline' over a small embankment towards the quarry, to reach the level area just below the spoil heap. Various bumps and gullies to the side of the tramway here indicate the site of a small community, where Templer built cottages, a pub and possibly a school for his workers. Later, in 1825, more cottages were built in Haytor Vale; the Rock Inn was originally the single-workers' hostel.

> **?** *How many sets of points can you find on this section of the granite tramway?*

The Rock Inn sign

Regain the flat area by the spoil heaps **A**, turn left and retrace your steps down the grassy path to the car park. ■

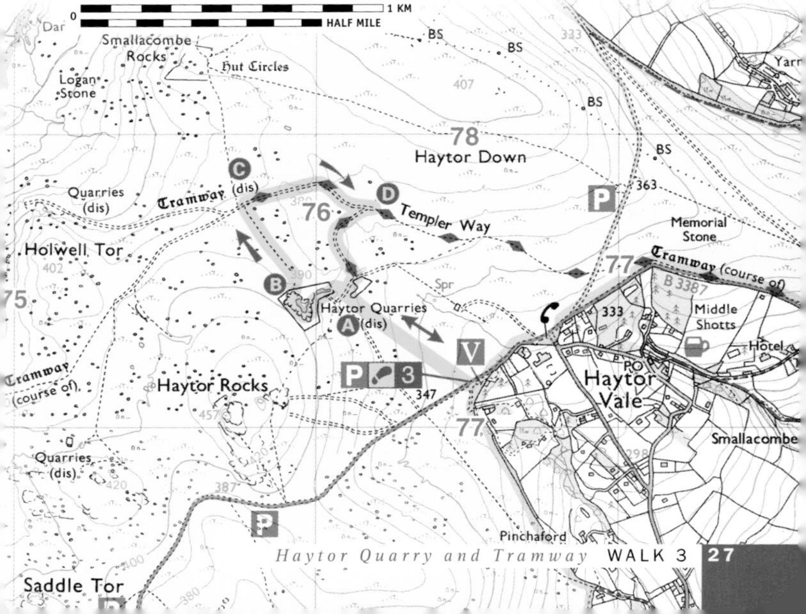

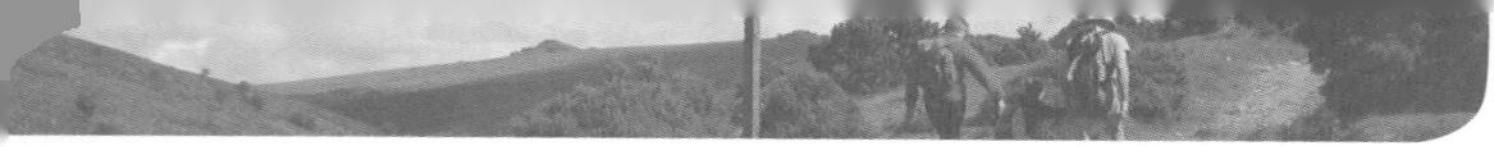

Hound Tor and Hayne Down

- Granite tors
- Jay's Grave
- Bowerman's Nose
- medieval village

walk 4

For views of the greatest number of tors in a small area, this has to be one of the best short walks on Dartmoor. It is also packed with all kinds of legends and stories, and ends at the ruined medieval village on Houndtor Down, best seen on a sunny day in May when the slopes are covered with a shimmering azure carpet of bluebells.

Climbers on Hound Tor

walk 4

START Hound Tor

DISTANCE 3½ miles (5.6km)

TIME 2 hours

PARKING Hound Tor car park at Swallerton Gate

ROUTE FEATURES Uneven rocky path from Hayne Down to Hayne; steep climb up the lane from Great Houndtor Farm to the cattle-grid

GPS WAYPOINTS
- Start SX 740 792
- A SX 732 799
- B SX 739 800
- C SX 751 807
- D SX 746 793
- E SX 745 788

PUBLIC TRANSPORT None available

REFRESHMENTS Mobile refreshments van ('Hound of the Basket Meals') in car park daily Easter–end September, and winter holidays and weekends

PUBLIC TOILETS None en route

PICNIC/PLAY AREA None

ORDNANCE SURVEY MAPS Explorer OL28 (Dartmoor), Landranger 191 (Okehampton & North Dartmoor)

Hound Tor 1,358ft (414m), rising craggily before the car park, is said to resemble a pack of hounds frozen in flight. Turn right along the lane; at Swallerton Gate turn right and walk past the thatched Dartmoor longhouse on the left, originally a pub. Ignore the small lane running off to the right (unsuitable for motor vehicles), and walk along the grassy bank on the right of the lane. Look left for views of Honeybag and Chinkwell Tors, and the swell of Hamel Down beyond. Jay's Grave is soon reached at the edge of beechwoods on the left; the pointed hill ahead in the distance is Easdon Tor.

> **Kitty Jay** was the daughter of a tenant farmer, who was betrayed by the son of a local landowner. When he refused to marry her she hanged herself, and was buried without ceremony at the cross-roads on Hayne Down. Years later, her bones were excavated and reburied in the simple grave that can be seen today. You will always find flowers here, sometimes said to be the work of a ghostly hand who refuses to let Kitty's sad story be forgotten.

A Turn right on the bridlepath through a small wooden gate and up the grassy slope, with the wire fence left. At the top of the hill amazing views of Dartmoor's tors open up. Pass through a small wooden gate, then a collapsed wall, and keep straight on with

Jay's Grave

the fence left. Note Haytor Rocks to the south, and the quarry at Holwell Tor; you can also pick out the line of the granite tramway along Haytor Down. Views towards Hayne Down open up ahead; look towards the left slope of the down to see the distinctive outline of Bowerman's Nose. Pass through another gate and keep ahead downhill, then through two more fields and gates, aiming for the bottom left corner of the last field; pass through a small wooden gate onto the lane.

> **Bowerman's Nose,** towering nearly 40ft (12.25m) high, is a natural feature – but local legend tells the story of an 11th-century hunter, Bowerman, who disturbed a coven of witches. In revenge, they encased him in stone, and although his family searched high and low they found no trace of him. There he stands to this day, regretting the folly of his ways.

B Turn left through Moyles Gate. Turn right up a grassy path (slightly boggy in winter); ignore a path that leads left towards Bowerman's Nose. Follow the path uphill, aiming for the saddle between the two rocky outcrops. Pass over the saddle nearer to the left outcrop, then follow the path downhill through bracken, with great views towards Manaton church (ahead left) and Hunter's Tor beyond the Bovey Valley. The path reaches a granite wall (left), and ends at a gate. Go through the gate and downhill through a wooded area to pass Hayne on the left, then down a tarmac drive to reach Hayne Cross.

C Turn right along the quiet lane to pass Southcott Farm. The lane undulates before dropping down to pass Great Houndtor Farm on the right, and then climbs very steeply up to the cattle-grid at the edge of Houndtor Down.

> **?** ***Where will you find Winnie the Pooh and Piglet on this walk?***

D Turn left along the narrow bridlepath (Black Hill and Haytor Down). At a crossroads of paths turn left **E** to reach the ruined medieval village, with Greator Rocks beyond – a great picnic spot. Originally the site of a Bronze Age settlement, the village may have been reoccupied around the 9th century, but was constructed of wood and turf. Retrace your steps to the crossroads and keep ahead uphill, making for Hound Tor. Pass to the left of the main outcrop, then straight downhill to the car park. ■

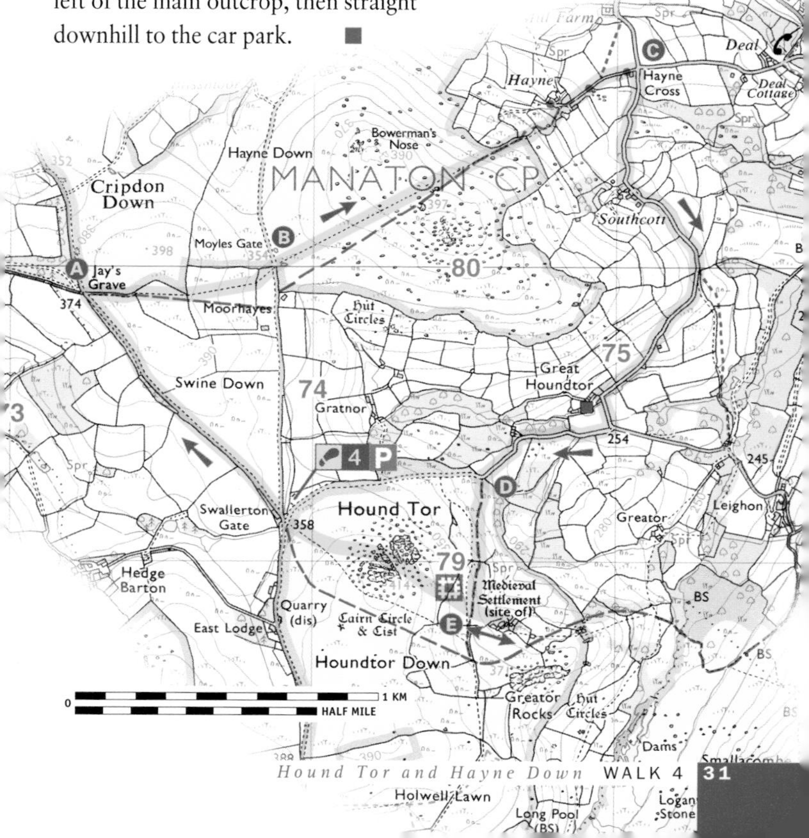

Lydford

- Medieval 'castle'
- Lych Way
- moorland views
- St Petrock's Church

walk 5

The pretty village of Lydford, nestling on the western edge of the moor, is a somewhat misleading place: in medieval times its prison, court and fearsome reputation for justice were legendary. This gentle walk touches on every aspect of the village's long and fascinating history, as well as taking in two pubs and skirting the edge of the open moor.

The Castle Inn, Lydford

walk 5

START Lydford

DISTANCE $2\frac{1}{4}$ miles (3.6km)

TIME 1 hour

PARKING Car park in the village

ROUTE FEATURES Quiet lanes and tracks; gradual ascent onto moorland edge

GPS WAYPOINTS
- Start: SX 510 848
- Ⓐ SX 513 850
- Ⓑ SX 521 846
- Ⓒ SX 522 852

PUBLIC TRANSPORT Bus service from Barnstaple, Okehampton, Plymouth, Tavistock

REFRESHMENTS The Castle Inn and Hotel, Lydford; Dartmoor Inn at the Lydford turning on the A386

PUBLIC TOILETS In the car park

PICNIC/PLAY AREA None

ORDNANCE SURVEY MAPS Explorer OL28 (Dartmoor), Landranger 191 (Okehampton & North Dartmoor)

Leave the car park and turn right. Just past the Nicholls Hall on the left, bear right along Silver Street, so named because Lydford was home to one of Devon's four mints in the time of Aethelred II (AD979–1026), producing silver pennies. Examples of these can be seen in the 16th-century Castle Inn, opposite the car park. Where the tarmac lane ends (private drive left) keep right and follow the gritty, sometimes muddy track downhill to reach a junction of paths Ⓐ.

> Just west of the village lies **Lydford Gorge**, cared for by the National Trust, and well worth a visit. The River Lyd runs through the $1\frac{1}{2}$ mile- (2.4km-) long gorge via a series of crashing waterfalls and whirlpools – the most impressive being the spectacular 30m (98ft) White Lady waterfall and the Devil's Cauldron – which can be seen from several lovely woodland walks. There is also a shop and café on the site.

A tarmac lane comes in from the left; the Lych Way comes in from the right. St Petrock's Church used to be the parish church for much of Dartmoor, and before AD1260 the dead were carried here for burial from as far away as the Postbridge district around 14 miles (22.5km) away. The route became known as the Lych Way (lich meaning corpse). Walk straight ahead, slightly uphill, to pass beneath the railway bridge (part of the Lydford Junction–Okehampton line, which operated from 1874–1968). At the next fork, keep right to pass between high hedges; the narrow path dips down to pass Kitts Cottage on the right, then runs up to meet the A386.

Lydford Castle

B Cross the road with care, and walk up the bridlepath opposite, which ends at a five-bar gate between granite gateposts. Walk through the gate to pass Highdown on the right, and onto open grassy moorland, with wonderful views of Doe Tor 1,394ft (425m) to the right. The Doetor Brook Valley, between Doe Tor and Brat Tor, is home to a wealth of tin-mining remains, based around the Wheal Frederick mine. Notice too, Brat Tor 1,483ft (452m) with a spectacular 13ft-(4m-) high cross on its summit. Instigated by the well-known Dartmoor artist F.J.Widgery, this commemorates Queen Victoria's Golden Jubilee in 1887. Follow the wall and line of beech trees on the left to pass along the edge of High Down; look out for views of Lydford village and castle to the left. The wall curves left; pass through a gate with a parking area

* A 'burh', or defended settlement, was created here in Saxon times, as part of a network to protect southern England from Viking raids. There are actually two castles at **Lydford**: a small Norman ringwork dating from around 1087, and the impressive freestanding tower, built in the late 12th century as a prison and courtroom. Lydford became the administrative centre for the old Forest of Dartmoor, and had jurisdiction over the stannary districts of Devon. The prison was used by the Royalists during the Civil War, and was abandoned by the late 17th century.

on the right. Follow the gritty track downhill and through another gate; walk on to reach the A386, just to the right of the Dartmoor Inn.

? *What is the inscription on the casing of the old drinking fountain which can be found near the driveway to Castle Lea and St Petrock's?*

C Cross the road (garage and shop to the right), and follow the lane opposite back into Lydford village, passing the Granite Way (cycle path) and the war memorial (at Rowell Cross) on the way. To take a look at St Petrock's Church, walk past the car park entrance and past the medieval 'castle'. The original Saxon church was probably constructed of wood; the first reference to a stone building dates to 1237, with restoration in the 15th and early 20th centuries. Dedicated to the Celtic saint St Petrock, who arrived in Cornwall in the 6th century, the church is famous for its superb woodcarvings and beautifully engraved tombstones, including that of George Routledge, a watchmaker who died in 1802: 'Wound up... In hopes of being taken in hand... By his Maker... And of being thoroughly cleaned, repaired... And set-going... In the world to come'. ■

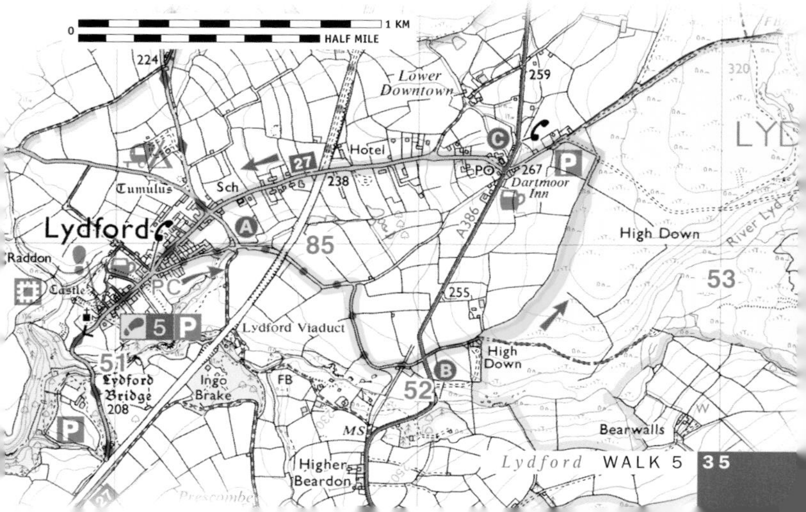

North and South Brentor

- Old railway
- rolling farmland
- moorland views
- Brent Tor church

walk 6

This walk provides a chance to explore the quiet westernmost corner of the Dartmoor National Park. The prominent landmark of Brent Tor church, perched on a rocky outcrop 1,000ft (335m) above sea level, is instantly recognisable for many miles around and is a fascinating place, both in terms of its geology and its legendary links with the Devil.

Brentor village hall

walk 6

START Gibbet Hill

DISTANCE 3 miles (4.8km) with possible 1½ mile (2.4km) extension

TIME 1½ hours (+ 1 hour)

PARKING In a lay-by on the left, 250 yds over the cattle-grid on the moorland lane between Mary Tavy and North Brentor

ROUTE FEATURES Rocky uneven descent to Wortha Mill; steep climb up to church (optional)

GPS WAYPOINTS

- (start) SX 493 800
- A SX 488 808
- B SX 481 814
- C SX 480 802
- D SX 472 800
- E SX 471 804

PUBLIC TRANSPORT Bus service from Okehampton and Tavistock (to Brent Tor) summer only; from Plymouth and Barnstaple (to North Brentor only) all year

REFRESHMENTS None en route; the Castle Inn at Lydford 2½ miles (4km) to the north

PUBLIC TOILETS None en route; in car park for Brent Tor church (plus information board)

PICNIC/PLAY AREA In North Brentor, signed right from the war memorial

ORDNANCE SURVEY MAPS Explorer 112 (Launceston & Holsworthy), Landranger 191 (Okehampton & North Dartmoor)

Cross over the lane from your car and keep ahead on a grassy path up the slopes of Gibbet Hill. Turn left at the path junction and follow this eventually downhill to meet the lane opposite two granite gateposts in the beech-lined wall (the entrance to Worthy Farm).

A Turn right along the lane, which drops down and bears left to reach a cattle-grid and wooden gate. Continue down the lane past the old railway station on the left. The lane crosses the disused railway line, then climbs uphill to pass Brentor village hall and Christ church (right). North Brentor was added to the parish of Brent Tor in 1880, after which date all burials took place in the village; it was very difficult to dig a deep enough grave on the top of Brent Tor. Walk on to reach the T-junction by the 1914–18 war memorial, with bus shelter opposite.

B Turn left. After a few yards the lane bends right. Bear left along Darke Lane to pass pretty cottages; the lane leads into a green lane signed 'South Brentor'. The green lane forks; keep left, and, where the lane sweeps to the right of a gate, follow the footpath sign through the gate. Walk straight on, keeping the hedgebank right, to pass through a gateway at the end of the field. Go straight across the next field, and through a small kissing-gate in the next hedge. Keep straight ahead and downhill to pass through another small kissing-gate, just by a ruined building (left). The next footpath sign points diagonally up the next field towards the top right corner. Leave the field over a small stile, and walk straight on, passing to the left of a gorse-studded embanked area (enclosing a muddy pond) to leave the field via a gate in the top right corner. Walk down the green lane, with great views to Brent Tor right, to meet another green lane at a T-junction near South Brentor Farm C.

Note: If you want to visit Brent Tor church turn right at C *and follow the lane until it bends sharp left; turn right* D *through a metal gate and walk steeply uphill towards the church, with hedge right. Pass through a gate at the top of the field and bear right round the hill, eventually climbing left up to the church* E.

* **Brent Tor** is not formed of granite; it is a remnant of the mass of lava that poured out onto the seabed here more than 300 million years ago. The church of St Michael de Rupe was built around 1130, with alterations in the 13th and 15th centuries, and is the fourth smallest complete parish church in England. Rumour has it that while the church was being built the Devil, displeased with what was going on, hurled stones from the top of the tor onto the unfortunate parishioners below – but he lost the battle.

If you don't want to visit the church turn left at C and follow the green lane steeply and rockily downhill between high banks. This section can be muddy in winter. The path crosses the River Burn and the old railway line via twin bridges – Wortha Mill Bridge – then runs uphill to pass restored Wortha Mill, a former corn-grinding mill, on the left. The track becomes tarmac at the entrance to Blacknor Park (right), then

Brent Tor church

leads over a cattle-grid to join the lane on the edge of Gibbet Hill. Turn right and walk along the lane to your car. ■

? *Somewhere near the church you will see a little spring bubbling out of a pipe, which used to supply the village with water. What is its date?*

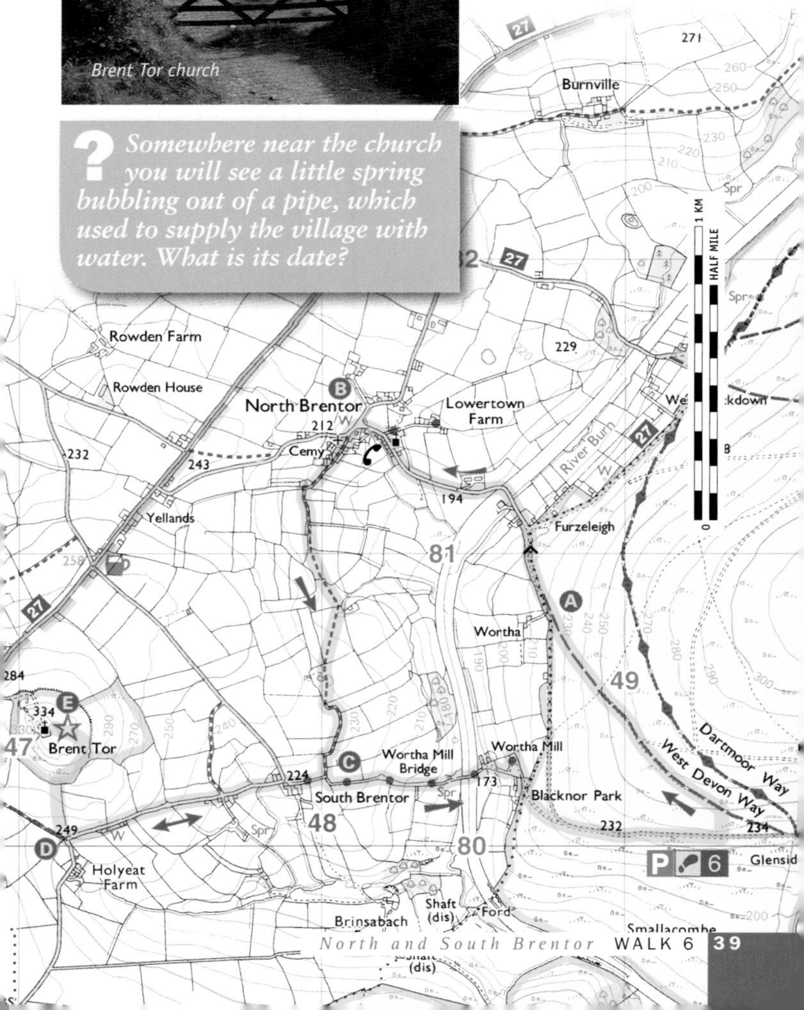

The Teign Gorge at Castle Drogo

- **Wooded gorge**
- **hill forts**
- **castle and gardens**
- **craggy tors**

walk 7

A gentle stroll along level paths high above the stunningly beautiful wooded River Teign gorge, with glorious views over Dartmoor. The walk leads below Castle Drogo, one of architect Sir Edwin Lutyens' finest works, set in a commanding position and famous as the 'youngest' castle in the country. The castle and estate are cared for by the National Trust.

Hunter's Path

walk 7

START Between Sandy Park and Castle Drogo

DISTANCE 2½ miles (4km)

TIME 1¼ hours

PARKING At the side of the lane opposite the entrance to Coombe Farm and Gibhouse

ROUTE FEATURES Good level path along top of gorge; dogs are not allowed into Castle Drogo and gardens

GPS WAYPOINTS
- SX 721 904
- Ⓐ SX 770 902
- Ⓑ SX 727 901
- Ⓒ SX 732 899
- Ⓓ SX 727 902
- Ⓔ SX 726 901

PUBLIC TRANSPORT Bus service from Okehampton, Newton Abbot and Exeter

REFRESHMENTS National Trust shop and café at the castle; also picnic area; Sandy Park Inn at Sandy Park

PUBLIC TOILETS By the café and shop

PICNIC/PLAY AREA By the picnic area

ORDNANCE SURVEY MAPS Explorer OL28 (Dartmoor), Landranger 191 (Okehampton & North Dartmoor)

Cross over the lane (which is very quiet) and turn right through a small gate next to a cattle-grid. Follow the concrete lane (signposted Hunter's and Fisherman's Paths) to the end of the field.

Ⓐ Where the lane becomes tarmac, turn left to leave it and pass through a small wooden gate under beech trees (signposted Hunter's Path). At this point you join a stretch of the Two Moors Way. *(Note: If you feel like a longer walk, you can go straight ahead here along the lane to reach the river, and then follow signs for the Fisherman's Path along the river to Fingle Bridge, and then take the Hunter's Path all the way back to the castle.)* At this point the walk enters the Castle Drogo estate. Follow the broad, level, flinty path along the valley

> * The **Teign gorge** was the site of significant activity long before Julius Drewe set about realising his dream. On the precipitously steep slopes above Fingle Bridge, a little farther down the gorge, lie Prestonbury Castle Iron Age hillfort, with its twin, Cranbrook Castle, on the hilltop opposite, built by Celtic peoples around 750BC–AD50.

side, with wonderful views opening up to the right, and Castle Drogo towering above you at the top of the bracken-covered slope on the left. The path bends sharply left at

Hunter's Tor to run above the Teign gorge; look ahead to see the craggy outcrop of Sharp Tor. Continue along the path, which falls very steeply away to the right; listen to the sounds of the river below as it rushes over rocks and boulders.

B Ignore a small flight of wooden steps on the left that lead up to the castle, and continue on to pass Sharp Tor; it is worth walking out onto the top of the outcrop, *but take great care.*

Continue on the main path; eventually turn left **C** up steps, then almost immediately left again (signed Castle Drogo and Piddledown Common). Keep straight on, with views of the castle opening up ahead, to pass along the Gorse Blossom Walk. Keep on the main path; at a fork after gateposts keep right to meet the main drive to the castle **D**. Turn left along the drive, and then right to gain the car park, café and shop. The castle was built between 1910 and 1930 with granite sourced locally from Blackenstone Quarry.

? *How many weirs cross the River Teign below the castle, and what are they called?*

***** It's well worth taking some time to explore **Castle Drogo**, which certainly fulfils Lutyens' ambition of combining the qualities and grandeur of a medieval castle with those of a comfortable 20th-century home (part of which is still inhabited) and the beautiful terraced formal gardens, designed in 1915. There is also a delightful woodland spring garden, with rhododendrons, azaleas and camellias, and an impressive circular yew-hedged croquet lawn.

Castle Drogo is one of Dartmoor's gems. Spectacularly situated high above the gorge of the Teign river, 1,000ft (305m) above sea level, it resulted from a successful collaboration between Sir Edwin Lutyens (1869–1944) and self-made millionaire Julius Drewe, who decided to establish his family seat here because he believed

Castle Drogo's main entrance

(mistakenly) that his ancestors had connections with the nearby village of Drewsteignton.

To return to your car, retrace your steps out of the car park and turn left along the drive; almost immediately (and before you reach the end of the Gorse Blossom Walk) turn right **E** (signed Estate Walks) down a narrow path. At the next footpath sign keep straight on downhill, then descend flights of wooden steps, to reach the Hunter's Path **B**.

Turn right and follow the path all the way back to your car, enjoying superb views towards Dartmoor. ■

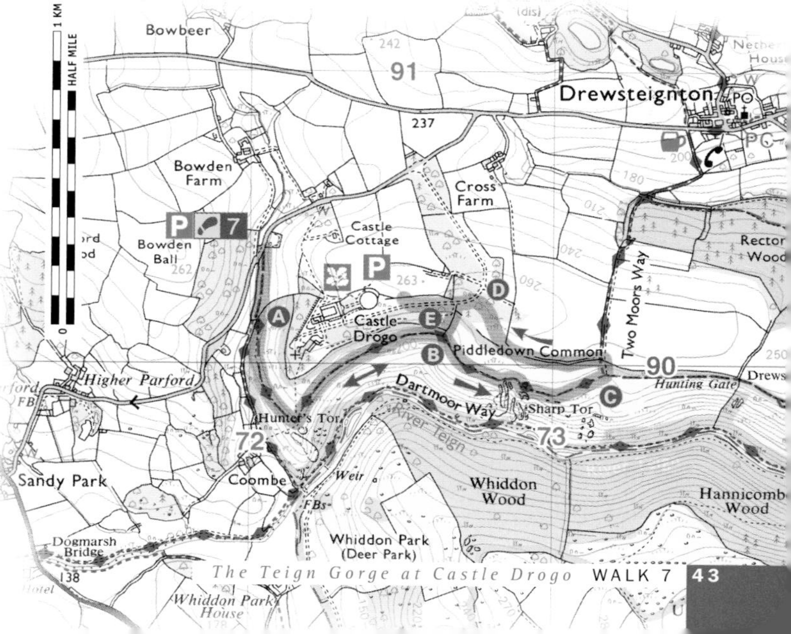

Trenchford and Tottiford Reservoirs

- Forest walks
- picnic sites
- rhododendrons
- lakeside birdlife

walk 8

This is a peaceful walk through quiet forests and around tranquil reservoirs – especially lovely in May when the rhododendrons are in bloom – that few people, even those who live relatively nearby, seem to know about. Situated well off the beaten track on the ridge between the Teign and Wray valleys, this is an ideal outing for anyone feeling less than energetic.

Tottiford Reservoir

walk 8

START Trenchford Reservoir

DISTANCE 2½ miles (4km)

TIME 1¼ hours

PARKING In the car park for Trenchford reservoir (contributions cairn) at Bullaton Cross

ROUTE FEATURES Woodland paths around reservoirs; no real ascents or descents. *Note that dogs should be kept on leads.*

GPS WAYPOINTS

- SX 804 824
- Ⓐ SX 803 829
- Ⓑ SX 803 834
- Ⓒ SX 807 836
- Ⓓ SX 810 833
- Ⓔ SX 810 826

PUBLIC TRANSPORT None available

REFRESHMENTS None en route; picnic areas by both Trenchford and Tottiford Reservoirs; the Cleave public house in Lustleigh south west of Trenchford Reservoir

PUBLIC TOILETS None

PICNIC/PLAY AREA None

ORDNANCE SURVEY MAPS Explorer OL44 (Torquay & Dawlish), Landranger 191 (Okehampton & North Dartmoor)

* **Tottiford** (completed 1861, and enlarged in 1866) and Kennick (1881–3) Reservoirs were constructed to meet the growing demand for water from the increasing populations of Newton Abbot and Torquay. Trenchford followed (1903–7) as a result of an exceptional drought in 1901. The underground water pipes supplying Torquay were kept clear by the use of a 'mole' that spiralled along inside them; runners kept track of the mole from the surface, listening hard to see if it got stuck.

From the information board follow the beaten earth path away from the car park under trees. The information board provides details of various walking routes – red, orange, and green – but this walk is going to be different from all of them. The path soon crosses a small wooden footbridge and runs along the edge of the water, with lovely views. Eventually, the path crosses a boardwalk, then bears right to cross the end of the reservoir on a narrow railed concrete bridge, to reach a T-junction of paths.

Ⓐ Turn left (signed Tottiford Reservoir walk). At the next T-junction of paths turn right uphill to pass through a peaceful larch plantation. This is a wonderful place; there is barely a sound as you pass over the thick carpet of needles, enjoying the resinous scent typical of such woodland. A small wooden path sign directs you left at the top of the hill along a level path, which then turns right through a spruce plantation to meet a lane at a gate.

* As well as providing great opportunities for walkers, the lakes also attract a large range of wildfowl, with heron, coot and cormorant all year round, and winter populations of **pochard, tufted duck, teal, goosander, Canada goose** and **mallard**. Kennick Reservoir also provides fishing (and is closed to walkers as a result).

B Cross the lane and pass through a gate; follow the path ahead, signed Tottiford Reservoir. Keep on the main path, following an orange arrow on a post. The path runs downhill with a mossy bank and beech trees left, and conifers right, and passes through another bank. Note glimpses of Tottiford Reservoir through the tree trunks ahead.

C Turn right at the water's edge. Follow the reservoir-side path, which soon becomes broader and grassy (look left to see the dam between Kennick and Tottiford Reservoirs). Eventually reach a footpath junction by a low, narrow fenced bridge across the water.

A peaceful woodland path

D Turn left and cross the bridge. Once on the other shore, turn right and thread your way along the narrow path around the left bank of the reservoir. Just before reaching the dam, bear left through the Tottiford Reservoir picnic area to meet a lane opposite a parking area. Turn right to meet a wider tarmac lane. *(To avoid returning along the lane turn right over the bridge, then left to pick up a path round the reservoir.)*

E Turn left and follow the lane along the side of Trenchford Reservoir to cross the dam, from where there are great views to the left over the treatment works. Just before the dam, take a moment to look at the granite plinth and a notice through an iron gate on the right, recording the building details and opening of the reservoir. Immediately over the dam, before the lane bends sharp right, turn right through a wooden gate onto a gritty path to pass a small works building and a plaque marking the feeder pipe from Fernworthy Reservoir on the high moor. Follow the path to pass through the picnic area and back to the car park. ■

> **?** *When was the supply of water from Fernworthy introduced to Trenchford Reservoir?*

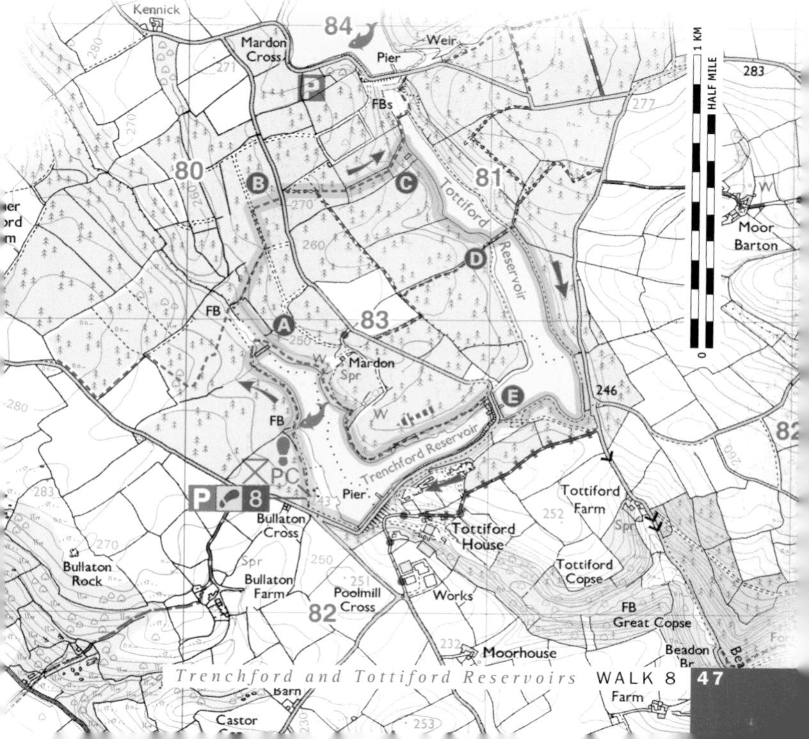

Avon Dam and Rider's Rings

- Waterfalls
- superb scenery
- Bronze Age site
- huge dam

walk 9

The Avon is one of Dartmoor's prettiest rivers, and the stretch just above Shipley Bridge is extremely popular with visitors. But you can quickly escape: having taken the easy route to the Avon Dam, this walk strikes out across the open moor to visit a Bronze Age settlement and a particularly well-sited tor, with stunning views across the valley and over south Devon.

By the Avon Dam

walk 9

START
Shipley Bridge

DISTANCE 4 miles (6.4km)

TIME 2 hours

PARKING Car park at Shipley Bridge (unmarked), signposted from South Brent

ROUTE FEATURES Tarmac lane then indistinct and rough walk across open moorland from Avon Dam to Rider's Rings

GPS WAYPOINTS
- SX 681 629
- Ⓐ SX 682 632
- Ⓑ SX 681 637
- Ⓒ SX 679 651
- Ⓓ SX 679 650
- Ⓔ SX 679 645
- Ⓕ SX 681 635

PUBLIC TRANSPORT None available

REFRESHMENTS None en route; picnic tables near Long-a-traw; range of pubs and cafés in South Brent

PUBLIC TOILETS Adjoining car park

PICNIC/PLAY AREA In car park

ORDNANCE SURVEY MAPS
Explorer OL28 (Dartmoor), Landranger 202 (Torbay & South Dartmoor)

An ancient route commonly known as the **Abbot's Way** runs along the northern edge of the reservoir, and leads from Buckfastleigh on the south east edge of the moor to Tavistock Abbey and Buckland Abbey on the west. Its alternative name is the Jobbers' Path, dating from medieval times. Dartmoor had an important wool industry from the mid-14th to late-15th centuries, and the route is thought to have been used for collecting wool and fleeces from the southern part of the moor.

Shipley Bridge car park is on the site of the former Brent Moor china clay works, as evidenced by the ruined buildings. Clay was brought here for processing via a wooden railed tramway from Redlake china clay workings in the middle of the southern moor.

Leave the car park and turn left; just before the bridge turn left up a tarmac lane signed Brockhill Ford and Abbot's Way, with the pretty Avon on the right. The longest of southern Dartmoor's rivers at 22 miles (35km), the Avon's source is at Aune Head, a huge mire. This river is particularly lovely here, with tumbling waterfalls and deep pools.

Ⓐ Where a small lane leads left to the Avon Water Treatment Works, note the large block of granite – the Hunter's Stone – to the left. This is a memorial to four

19th-century South Devon Hunt masters, and was engraved by C.A. Mohun-Harris, former occupant of Brent Moor House, the crenellated gateposts of which are passed a little farther up the lane. About 50 yds (46m) beyond the gateposts there is a memorial on a rock to the left of the path, to a girl who died hereabouts in 1863. Opinions vary as to whether she drowned or died in a riding accident. The ruins of Brent Moor House are soon passed on the left. Originally the hunting lodge of the Meynell family, the house became a youth hostel before being demolished in 1968.

B The lane crosses the Avon over a bridge to enter open moorland; 275 yds (250m) later there is a picnic area on the right. Follow the lane as it wends its way towards the Avon Dam, which eventually can be seen ahead, blocking the valley. This part of the Avon is known as Long-a-traw, on account of its route through a moorland trough. Just before reaching the dam, the lane bears left to cross the river again on a granite bridge.

C Turn left to leave the lane up a steep gritty path to reach the left end of the dam; just over the other side there is a good picnic spot at the water's edge. At times of drought the remains of a medieval farmstead may be seen on the north east side. The slopes around the reservoir are bare; most of Dartmoor's reservoirs are surrounded by plantations. The dam was built between 1955–7, to supply water to Totnes and the South Hams. Retrace your steps back to the lane.

Walk down the lane: about 100 yds (91m) before the bridge, bear right **D** over a rocky area to pick up a narrow path along the slope of a grassy plateau, avoiding a boggy area near the river. Drop down to cross Zeal Gully and stream; ahead you will see two indistinct rough paths through the bracken on the hill. Keep to the right-hand path; at the top of the hill the path levels out to meet a break in the outer wall of Rider's Rings.

E Turn right and follow the wall to its end; walk straight on and after 250 yds (228m) turn left and pick your way across a stream. Walk straight ahead, keeping high along the contours of Zeal Hill, before bearing left to Black Tor, which soon becomes visible. This is a wonderfully open, grassy route. The views from Black Tor 1,050ft (320m) are superb; look over the valley to Shipley Tor 984ft (300m), and south over the South Hams towards the sea.

F From the middle of Black Tor pick your way downhill towards the valley, towards a granite wall. About 20 yds (18m) from the wall bear left and follow the path downhill, parallel to the wall at first. The path descends and forks; take the right fork to reach the lane by the enclosure wall. Turn right to retrace your steps to your car. ■

* Larger and more remote than its more famous counterpart, Grimspound, **Rider's Rings** is an enclosed early prehistoric settlement. Divided into two areas, the remains of 34 huts and numerous enclosures have been found within the outer wall.

? *What are you not allowed to do in the reservoir; and what can you do?*

Bonehill Rocks

- Dramatic tors
- moorland views
- Widecombe village
- pretty inns

walk 10

A lovely, airy route along the tops of four impressive tors – Bonehill Rocks, Bell, Chinkwell and Honeybag Tors – overlooking the classic Dartmoor village of Widecombe in the Moor, easily recognised from countless postcards and calendars. Widecombe is best visited on foot, and this walk offers a route that largely avoids the crowds – and takes in an excellent pub.

Granite formations on Bell Tor

walk 10

START Between Haytor and Widecombe in the Moor

DISTANCE 3½ miles (5.6km) with possible 1¾ mile (3.8km) extension

TIME 1¾ hours (+ 1 hour)

PARKING Unmarked hilltop car park on the north side of the B3387 east of Widecombe

ROUTE FEATURES Rocky paths between the tors; steep walk down and back through Bonehill (extension)

GPS WAYPOINTS
- SX 735 768
- Ⓐ SX 732 774
- Ⓑ SX 731 776
- Ⓒ SX 729 785
- Ⓓ SX 723 785
- Ⓔ SX 721 769
- Ⓕ SX 721 765

PUBLIC TRANSPORT Bus service from Buckfastleigh, Newton Abbot, Okehampton, Totnes, Tavistock

REFRESHMENTS None on main route; the Rugglestone Inn, the Old Inn, Café on the Green and Wayside Café in Widecombe

PUBLIC TOILETS None on main route; in the main car park in Widecombe

PICNIC/PLAY AREA On the Natsworthy Gate lane out of Widecombe

ORDNANCE SURVEY MAPS Explorer OL28 (Dartmoor), Landranger 191 (Okehampton & North Dartmoor)

? How steep is the lane leading down from Bonehill Rocks towards Widecombe?

With your back to the road follow a broad grassy path towards Bonehill Rocks 1,289ft (393m), which can be seen ahead with Bell Tor beyond and above. The path eventually passes a big granite boulder before dropping downhill. Bear right on approaching the tor to cross a stream Ⓐ (often dry in summer) just below a small parking area. Bonehill Rocks is a great place for children, who love to explore its nooks and crannies. The views from here are stunning, and the one over Widecombe in the Moor, nearly 500ft (166m) below, is one of Dartmoor's most famous.

From Ⓐ pass to the right of the rocks on a grassy path that runs anti-clockwise round the tor to reach another parking area Ⓑ. Turn right to cross the lane (note a pair of granite gateposts left) and walk along a gritty track. Almost immediately the track bears left, following a wall; just past a gate in the wall bear right uphill on a grassy path that leads to Bell Tor 1,312ft (400m), from where there are wonderful views south east to Haytor, Saddle Tor and Rippon Tor.

Follow the grassy path north and uphill along the top of the ridge to gain the two piles of Chinkwell Tor 1,503ft (458m), the second of which is crowned by two cairns. The path then dips down to cross a path junction **C** and up again to reach the strangely shaped rock piles of Honeybag Tor 1,460ft (445m), from which there are glorious views of the sea at Teignmouth to the south, Hound Tor to the east, and of Hamel Down over the cultivated East Webburn river valley to the west.

Retrace your steps to the saddle between Honeybag and Chinkwell Tors, crossing the embanked gully en route. William Crossing noted a line of manorial boundary stones here, in the region marked 'Slades Well', and there are remains of Bronze Age hut circles, too. Turn right **C** down a broad grassy path that leads off the ridge to meet a level gritty track, formerly a carriage drive. Turn left **D** and follow the track to reach the lane by Bonehill Rocks.

To return to your car cross straight over the lane, walk through the lower edge of the car park **B** and pass round the right side of the tor. Keep going to find the stream crossing below the parking area **A**, cross over and retrace your steps along one of the many grassy paths leading back to the car park.

> * **Widecombe Fair**, originally an important livestock market, is today a highly commercialised affair, held on the second Tuesday of September. The popular ballad woven around the story of *Uncle Tom Cobley 'n' all* tells of how Tom Pearce's grey mare made her way to Widecombe Fair carrying six individuals, and was (not surprisingly) ridden to her death. She is said to haunt the local moor to this day. The event is commemorated in relief on the granite parish sign near the village green.

Note: If you feel like a drink at the Rugglestone Inn, turn right at **B** *and walk steeply downhill through the peaceful hamlet of Bonehill. At the end of the lane turn left* **E** *and almost immediately right over a stile (signed public footpath); at the end of that field cross a wooden stile and iron railings and turn left; the pub* **F** *is within 100 yds (91m). The Rugglestone has a pretty garden, with a stream. After lunch, walk straight back along the lane into the village past the church, 15th-century Church House and Sexton's Cottage (NT). A shop and information centre can be found in the Church House. Turn right along the road opposite the 14th-century Old Inn, to pass the green, and take the next lane left to retrace your steps up the hill to reach point* **B** *again, by Bonehill Rocks.* ■

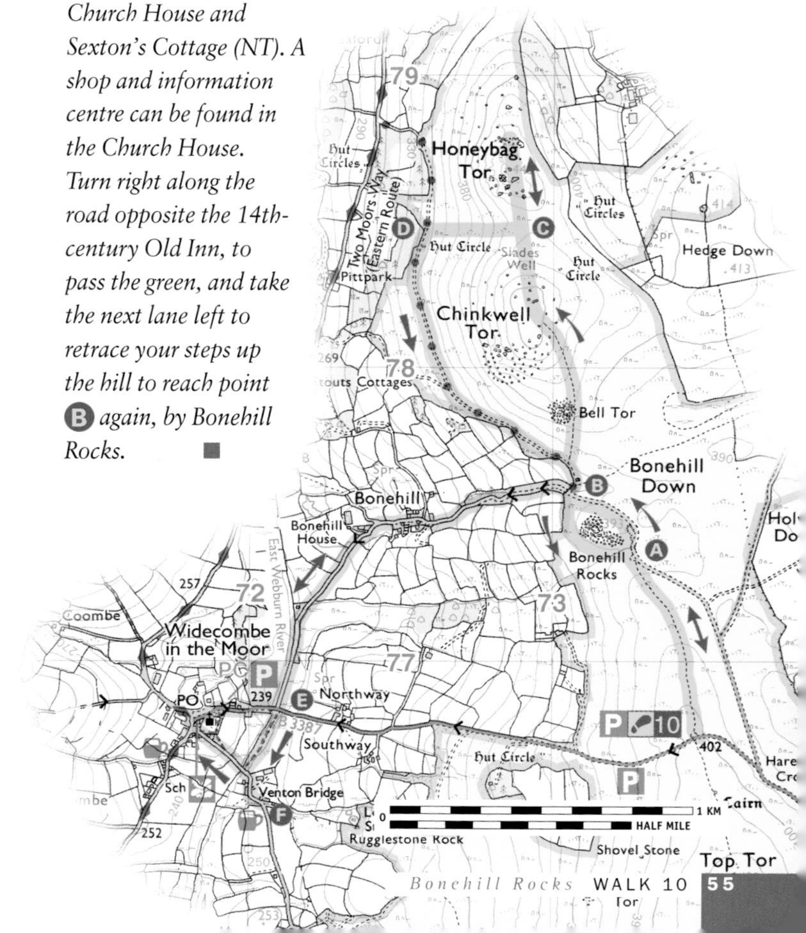

Crazywell Pool

- Moorland pool
- forest paths
- Devonport Leat
- aqueduct

walk 11

A wonderfully varied walk, starting and ending through the peaceful forest plantations around Burrator Reservoir. The middle section crosses the open moor and takes in mysterious Crazywell Pool, home to a wealth of legends, before following the Devonport Leat as it tumbles down Raddick Hill to cross the River Meavy on a little aqueduct.

Crazywell Pool

walk 11

START
Norsworthy Bridge, signposted from Burrator Reservoir dam

DISTANCE $3\frac{1}{2}$ miles (5.6km)

TIME 2 hours

PARKING Parking area near Norsworthy Bridge

ROUTE FEATURES Woodland tracks, rough moorland; steep rocky downhill path to the River Meavy

GPS WAYPOINTS
- (start) SX 569 693
- A SX 568 694
- B SX 579 701
- C SX 582 702
- D SX 584 706
- E SX 573 714
- F SX 565 697

PUBLIC TRANSPORT None available

REFRESHMENTS None en route; Royal Oak pub at Meavy south west of Burrator Reservoir; many good picnic spots around Burrator Reservoir

PUBLIC TOILETS None en route; by reservoir dam

PICNIC/PLAY AREA None

ORDNANCE SURVEY MAPS
Explorer OL28 (Dartmoor), Landranger 202 (Torbay & South Dartmoor)

There are various parking spaces around Norsworthy Bridge; park in the main one as indicated on the map. Walk towards the bridge, over the stream.

A As the lane bends sharp left to cross the bridge turn right up a rough wooded track, with lovely old granite walls. After a few minutes a T-junction of tracks is reached;

> **?** *Which three animal footprints are represented in colour on the wooden posts found near the start and end of the walk?*

Norsworthy Plantation is to the left. Turn right, to follow the track slightly uphill and along the edge of the plantation. Views of Down Tor 1,135ft (346m) open up to the right. At the next junction of paths, Raddick Lane joins from the left; keep walking right on the main track. The trees of Raddick Plantation gradually become thinner as the track reaches a wooden gate that leads onto the open moor. Newleycombe Lake (the valley below right) has a wealth of old tin-mining remains.

B Once through the gate, look back for great views over Burrator Reservoir, which covers 150 acres (60.75ha) and was constructed from 1891–8 to supply water to Plymouth. Enlarged in 1928, it has a capacity of 1,026 million gallons (4,572 million litres), and replaced Drake's Leat. The surrounding forests were first planted in 1921. Continue up the track; where a spring crosses the path turn left **C** up a narrow path onto grassy moorland, just to the right of a deep gully. Note a restored stone cross on the horizon ahead and slightly to the right. Follow the gully and within a few minutes Crazywell Pool is reached.

Skirt around the right edge of the pool, then walk straight ahead from the top corner across the moor towards some blocks of dressed granite, which are lying just by the Devonport Leat. Cross the leat over the stone slab bridge.

> * **Crazywell Pool** is a flooded mineworking, but its remote location has given rise to all kinds of legends and superstitions. Some believe it to be tidal, linked to the sea at Plymouth by a huge tunnel; some think it is bottomless; but the most eerie tale relates to a wailing voice that calls out the name of the next person to die in the parish of Walkhampton... and on Midsummer's Eve the reflection of that person can be seen in the dark waters of the pool.

D Turn left and follow the leat along its right bank, passing a sluice gate (used to divert water out of the leat if the flow was too heavy), two more stone slab bridges, and later another sluice gate. This path is boggy in places, and becomes rockier as the steep descent off Raddick Hill is made. Follow the leat as it rushes down to cross the River Meavy on a small aqueduct **E**, built in 1792. The path leads over metal rails at each end of the aqueduct. As the leat bends sharp left, note the feeder pipe bringing in water from the Hart Tor Brook. The Meavy Valley to the right here is rich in Bronze Age and tin-working remains; this is a great picnic spot.

Follow the leat on, keeping to the right bank: a level and very easy walk after clambering over the open moor. The leat loops left to pass under the wall of Stanlake Plantation. Note the ruins of Stanlake

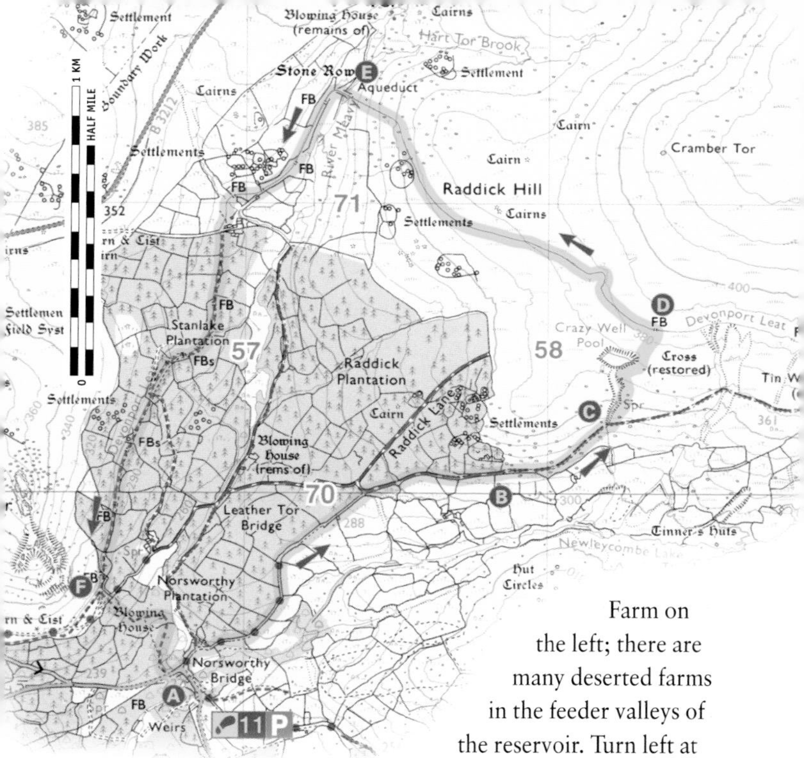

Farm on the left; there are many deserted farms in the feeder valleys of the reservoir. Turn left at the wall, then right through a gate into the plantation (signed Crossgate and Yennadon). The leat is wonderfully quiet here, and the forest light and open; see if you can spot any brown trout in the waters. At the next junction of paths, Leather Tor Farm is signed left; keep walking straight on along the leat. The clitter of Leather Tor (1,181ft/360m) is visible through the trees to the right. The path drops down and passes through a gate. About 75 yds (70m) later bear left F downhill to leave the leat (although it is very tempting to keep following it at this point). The next footpath sign directs you left for Norsworthy Bridge down a narrow path that crosses a track; then through a gate and downhill through trees. The path ends at a wooden gate onto the lane; turn left to cross Norsworthy Bridge and back to the car. ■

The East and West Okement Rivers

- Okehampton Castle
- waterfalls
- beech woods
- stepping stones

walk 12

The old market town of Okehampton on the northern fringe of Dartmoor (bypassed by the A30) is full of surprises. Within minutes of leaving the town you enter the lovely wooded valley of the East Okement River; then cross farmland overlooking Dartmoor's highest tors before descending through beech woods surrounding romantic Okehampton Castle.

Okehampton Castle ruins

walk 12

START
Okehampton

DISTANCE 4½ miles (7.2km)

TIME 2¾ hours

PARKING Fee-paying car park in Mill Road, off East Street, Okehampton

ROUTE FEATURES
Occasionally rocky and narrow path by East Okement River; short yet steep climb through Halstock Wood

GPS WAYPOINTS
- SX 590 951
- Ⓐ SX 592 949
- Ⓑ SX 603 948
- Ⓒ SX 607 936
- Ⓓ SX 602 938
- Ⓔ SX 593 939
- Ⓕ SX 587 943
- Ⓖ SX 585 944

PUBLIC TRANSPORT Bus services from Barnstaple, Exeter, Newton Abbot, Plymouth, Torquay, Totnes

REFRESHMENTS Good range of pubs and cafés in Okehampton

PUBLIC TOILETS In car park

PICNIC/PLAY AREA None

ORDNANCE SURVEY MAPS
Explorer OL28 (Dartmoor), Landranger 191 (Okehampton & North Dartmoor)

Pass to the left of the toilets at the far end of the car park, then bear left on a walkway to reach Mill Road. Turn right and almost immediately left to cross the road and go up steps by the mill and waterwheel.

> **Okehampton Castle** is the largest castle in Devon, and was built by the Norman sheriff of Devon, Baldwin de Brionne, soon after 1066, although much of what remains today dates from the 13th and 15th centuries. The castle has been used as a strategic garrison over the centuries, and encouraged the development of Okehampton as an important market town for the area. For many generations it was owned by the Courtenay family, one time Earls of Devon, and today is under the care of English Heritage.

Turn right along the next lane, soon signed to 'Ball Hill and Father Ford'. This is part of the 90-mile (145km) Dartmoor Way, and also the Tarka Trail, which runs for 180 miles (290km) from Okehampton to the north coast and Exmoor. Follow the lane (with a leat on the left) to its end by Okehampton College playing fields' car park.

> ? *What animal paw print is used to mark the route of the Tarka Trail, and why?*

Ⓐ Walk through a five-bar gate; follow the path through three fields/ three kissing-gates to cross a tarmac track. Pass through a five-bar gate to enter Ball Hill conservation area. This is a beautiful wooded path – note the leat and sluice gate by the stream on the right – and ends at a five-bar gate onto a lane.

B Turn right; pass Molcote (right); go through a gate, under the railway viaduct, then turn right to cross the East Okement River via a railed wooden bridge. Turn left through a five-bar gate, following signs for the East Okement Valley, and under the A30 viaduct. Keep on the right bank of the river, signed Chapel Ford and the moor. The river is a delight, tumbling over granite boulders and providing excellent picnic spots; the intrusive A30 is quickly left behind. The path crosses granite stepping stones (wet in winter), and crosses a stream to enter West Cleave. Pass through an old granite wall to regain the river where it runs narrowly through broad granite pavements. Continue along the right bank; at a waterfall, the route climbs steeply over a rocky outcrop before levelling off.

The East Okement River

As the path drops downhill towards Chapel Ford, turn sharp right by a footpath post **C** and walk uphill through Halstock Wood. The path meets a stock fence and runs right through bracken and hazel, with great views right. Pass through a five-bar gate and granite gateposts, and on through bracken and rowan above the wooded Moor Brook Valley (right). A bank/fence comes in from the left; keep it on the left and proceed to a signpost.

D Turn right downhill; pick your way down to the Moor Brook, and over the stepping stones. Turn left along a narrow path through woodland and over a stile; cross the next stile into a field. Keep along the right edge (wall) and pass through a gate onto a lane. Turn

> ***** The **London and South Western Railway** line reached Okehampton in 1871. The line was extended on to Lydford in 1874 via the Meldon viaduct, climbing to 950ft (290m) above sea level at Prewley summit en route (the highest point on any Southern Region railway system), and on to Tavistock in 1876. The line closed for passengers in 1968. Today a walking and cycling route, the Granite Way, utilises part of the old railway line.

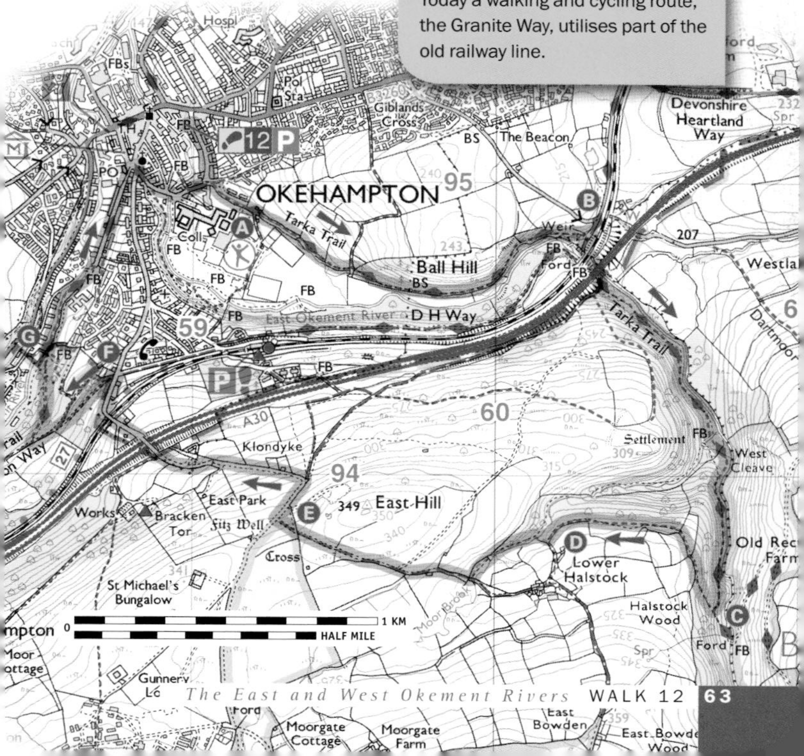

Below Ball Hill

right up the lane, which leads up along the edge of East Hill, with great views of Dartmoor's highest tors, and the army camp, built in the early 1880s. The army has used Dartmoor for training since the Napoleonic wars in the early 19th century, and now uses about one third of the open moor. The lane ends at a cattle-grid by a lane.

E Turn right; follow the road downhill over the A30 and railway. As houses are reached turn left **F** through a kissing-gate and follow a woodland path to reach a lane. Bear left along the lane for around 200 yds (182m) then turn sharp right downhill, signed 'castle and Okehampton'. The path drops down to meet a double-railed footbridge over the West Okement River.

G *Cross the bridge for the castle.* To continue the walk do not cross the bridge but keep ahead along a narrow path by the river, soon passing the old hospital. At the road turn right to pass Brock's Almshouses (1847). At the end of the lane cross the road, and turn right in front of Fairplace church. Pass Simmons Park and Okehampton College on the right. Just over the pedestrian crossing turn left and then right to find the car park. ■

Foggintor and Swelltor Quarries

- Moorland tracks
- tramways
- granite quarries
- industrial archaeology

Nearly 200 years ago this rather remote part of the moor was buzzing with industrial activity, brought about by one man's ultimately misguided dream of creating a prosperous community at Princetown. The walk follows part of the line of the old iron railway, opened in 1823, linking Princetown with Plymouth.

walk 13

Ruined buildings near Foggintor Quarry

walk 13

START
Just west of Princetown

DISTANCE 3½ miles (5.6km)

TIME 1½ hours

PARKING Small parking area just off track to Yellowmeade Farm, on the B3357

ROUTE FEATURES Brief rocky scramble around the edge of a gully at Swelltor Quarry

GPS WAYPOINTS
- SX 567 750
- A SX 566 737
- B SX 565 734
- C SX 562 731
- D SX 556 734

PUBLIC TRANSPORT Bus service (to Princetown) from Exeter, Newton Abbot, Plymouth, Tavistock, Totnes

REFRESHMENTS None en route; pubs and cafés in Princetown; also the Dartmoor Inn at Merrivale just west on the B3357

PUBLIC TOILETS None on route

PICNIC/PLAY AREA None

ORDNANCE SURVEY MAPS Explorer OL28 (Dartmoor), Landranger 191 (Okehampton & North Dartmoor)

Walk away from the road down the gritty track, signed Yellowmeade Farm (private road). Look ahead and, to the right, pick out the line of the old railway line as it runs beneath King's Tor 1,263ft (385m), and large spoil heaps ahead, indicating the edge of Foggintor granite quarries. As Yellowmeade Farm is approached, take the track that runs left of the farmhouse, and follow that to reach the edge of Foggintor Quarries.

> There are clear views of **Merrivale Quarry** from the old railway line. Originally known as Tor Quarry, this operated from 1875 to 1997, and was the last working quarry on Dartmoor. Granite blocks from the old London Bridge were re-dressed here when the bridge was sold to the USA, and stone was also used in the war memorial in the Falklands after the war in 1982. Watch out for the famous prehistoric Merrivale stone rows on the valley slopes as you look across to the quarry.

A Swelltor and Foggintor Quarries operated from around 1820, in direct competition with George Templer's quarries at Haytor. Foggintor (originally known as Royal Oak Quarry) ceased working around 1900, and Swelltor in 1921, although both quarries reopened in 1937 in response to an increase in demand for road building materials. Foggintor supplied granite for Dartmoor prison, and local granite was used in Nelson's Column in Trafalgar Square. There are masses of ruined buildings to the side of the quarries here, including (on the right of the path) the site of a chapel, also used as a school. Walk left down the narrow cleft that leads to the flooded quarry: it is wonderfully peaceful and sheltered, and a great picnic spot. Returning to the main track, continue walking through the workings, keeping the quarry on the left. At the end of the quarry there are views to the sea at Plymouth Sound ahead.

> **?** *What do you think the 12 blocks of dressed granite lying by the track near King's Tor might have been used for?*

B As the track curves left, turn right and follow the path over the disused embanked railway track

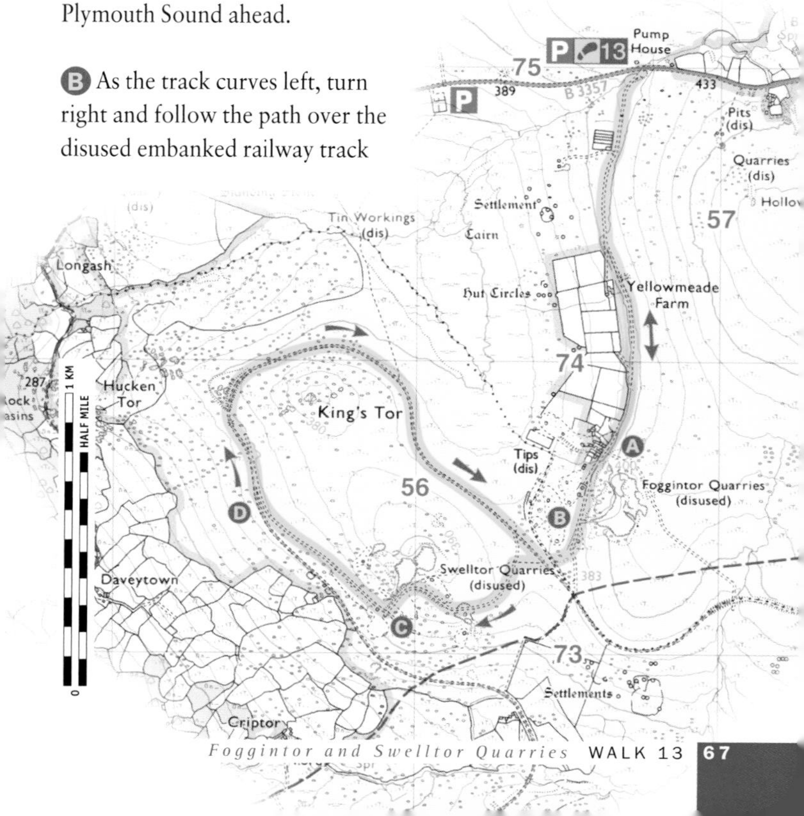

(near the site of King Tor Halt, dating from 1928, from where a siding called Royal Oak led to Foggintor). Walk ahead up the grassy path; this is crossed by two tracks, both of which are visible as you approach them. Turn left on the first of these and follow it along the contours of the hill to gain Swelltor Quarries, where the path ends at a deep gully and spoil heaps; *pick your way carefully around the right edge of this.*

> * The **Plymouth and Dartmoor Railway** was the brainchild of Sir Thomas Tyrwhitt, and ran for just over 25 miles (40km) across the moors and through farmland. After the Napoleonic wars granite was much in demand for building works, and Tyrwhitt seized the opportunity to exploit the area's natural resources, at the same time enabling materials such as coal and lime to be brought to Princetown more easily. The Princetown Railway Company (subsidiary of the GWR) took over the line in 1881; it reopened as a steam railway in 1883, but was never profitable and closed in 1956.

C Pick up the quarry siding on the other side, and follow this easy, level route around the contours of the hill towards King's Tor. The track reaches an area of ruined buildings and old workings by King's Tor Quarry, overlooking the wooded valley of the River Walkham, with great views of Vixen Tor 1,024ft (312m) beyond. Thought to be home to one of the moor's most evil characters, the witch Vixana, Vixen Tor is the tallest tor on Dartmoor, standing almost 100ft (30m) high. Note the grass-covered wooden sleepers on the track. Just after the quarry you will come across 12 corbels lying at the side of the track, which then drops gently down to meet the disused Plymouth and Dartmoor railway line.

D Follow the old line around the hill, and over a high embankment with a granite bridge beneath. Follow this easy, elevated line until it reaches the point at which it was crossed on the outward route **B**; turn left uphill to regain the track at Foggintor Quarries. Turn left and retrace your steps to the car. ■

Scorhill

- Stone circle
- Kes Tor
- clapper bridges
- castle ruin

This varied walk is full of natural and man-made features that span many thousands of years: stone circles, clapper bridges, a tolmen stone, one of the deepest rock basins on a Dartmoor tor, Bronze Age and Iron Age settlements, a medieval path that crossed the whole of Devon, an ancient church and a ruined castle.

walk **14**

The Tolmen Stone

walk 14

START Moor gate at Scorhill

DISTANCE 4½ miles (7.2km)

TIME 2¼ hours

PARKING Unmarked parking area at end of lane; Scorhill is signposted from Gidleigh

ROUTE FEATURES Rough moorland for first half of walk; steep woodland path down to River Teign and back up through Gidleigh Woods

GPS WAYPOINTS
- SX 661 877
- (A) SX 665 874
- (B) SX 665 871
- (C) SX 666 863
- (D) SX 669 873
- (E) SX 672 882
- (F) SX 664 879

PUBLIC TRANSPORT None available

REFRESHMENTS None en route; Northmore Arms at Wonson north of Gidleigh; several pubs and cafés in Chagford

PUBLIC TOILETS None en route

PICNIC/PLAY AREA None

ORDNANCE SURVEY MAPS Explorer OL28 (Dartmoor), Landranger 191 (Okehampton & North Dartmoor)

* **Scorhill stone circle** is nearly 90ft (27.5m) in diameter and comprises more than 30 stones, the tallest around 8ft (2.5m) high, and probably dates from the early Bronze Age. Many similar circles on the moor have been restored, but Scorhill has not, although some stones have been removed and used to line the leat a little farther downhill. Dartmoor has a wealth of Bronze Age remains, and the many standing stones, stone circles and stone rows are thought to have some kind of ritual significance.

Walk through the wooden gate onto the moor, and uphill on the broad grassy path. Where the granite wall to the left bears away keep straight on up the slightly sunken path. As you reach the crest of the hill Kestor Rock can be seen ahead and left, beyond the conifers fringing Batworthy. As you descend, the path splits; keep right to reach Scorhill stone circle.

(A) Turn left at the circle and walk downhill, aiming for the point at which the conifers drop into the valley of the Teign River. En route, the path crosses a small leat; nearer the river the way becomes rocky and uneven, but leads directly to the Tolmen Stone, a large granite block with a hole through it, created by the eroding force of the water. The stone is lodged high above the river, shifted from its original

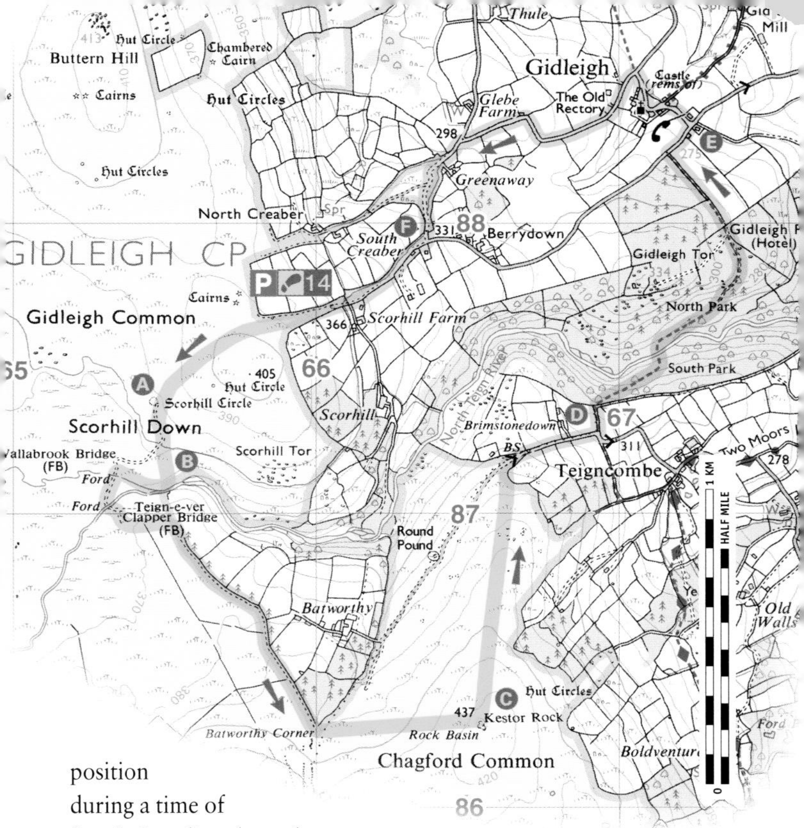

position during a time of flood. Crawling through such a hole was once thought to cure rheumatism, or whooping cough in children – and many people venture through the Tolmen Stone today, just in case.

B Turn right and walk up river, then left over the Walla Brook clapper bridge, then keep ahead to cross the Teign on Teign-e-ver clapper bridge. Walk straight ahead uphill, keeping the wall and conifers around Batworthy on your left; parts of this can be muddy. Follow the wall until it bends very sharply left; as you round the corner, Kestor Rock 1,434ft (437m) is directly ahead. Clamber to the top of the rocks, from where there are fantastic views in all directions. Look for the water-filled rock basin on the top, which, when cleared out in 1856, was railed off to prevent sheep from drowning. Thought to be the deepest such basin on the moor (and a natural feature), in Victorian times it was said to be used to catch blood from those unfortunates sacrificed by Druids.

* There is extensive evidence of **Bronze Age** and **Iron Age** occupation to the north of **Kestor Rock**, in the form of field systems (reaves – field boundaries) and hut circles. Iron Age remains are unusual on the moor; climatic deterioration before that time caused much of it to become depopulated, but cultivation continued at this site on the drier, eastern side. Near the lane (see map) there is a round pound, possibly a smithy, dating from around 500BC, with the remains of a hut within its own enclosure.

C From Kestor turn left and walk along the top of the ridge, with wooded Batworthy to the left, and a wall and woodland in the valley right. This leads you through the area of Bronze Age and later Iron Age settlement, originating from around 1500BC. At the end of the ridge drop down left to meet a lane, and turn right downhill through a gate by a cattle-grid.

D Around 100 yds (91m) along the lane turn left down a rough track, signed Gidleigh, and over a stile. Follow the path downhill and right; then turn left and descend steeply through a coniferous plantation to meet the Teign at Glassy Steps, which is crossed via a double-railed wooden footbridge. This is on the route of the Mariner's Way, thought to date from medieval times, which ran from Dartmouth, on the south coast, to Bideford on the north. Once over the river you meet a track; follow the signs right through North Park (Gidleigh Woods). The next path sign directs you sharp left; having turned, bear right and head steeply uphill. As the conifers thin out at the top the path levels off and crosses a gritty area; follow the signs along a track between granite walls to meet a lane at a gate and stile.

Kestor Rock

E Turn right downhill, and left at the next junction (Gidleigh Cross) by Gidleigh village hall. Walk on to find 15th-century Gidleigh church – Holy Trinity – a very pretty, simple granite building, with a wonderful line of 17th-/18th-century headstones against the outer wall. The graveyard is a carpet of snowdrops in February. Just beyond the church look through the iron gates of Gidleigh Castle, a fortified manor house built by Sir William Prous around AD1300. The ruined keep can be seen clearly; now privately owned, it is occasionally open to the public. Follow the lane uphill to a T-junction; turn left uphill, then later left again (signed Creaber and Scorhill). Where the lane bends sharp left (signed Gidleigh and Berrydown) turn right **F** opposite Cherryford House and walk up the lane to the car park. ■

? Find the west window in the church. In whose memory was it restored?

The Dewerstone

- Stone bridges
- granite crags
- wooded river valley
- extensive views

walk 15

This is a popular walk that can easily be done in either direction. There is a mass of interest here: the Plym at Cadover Bridge is great for paddling and picnics; Shaugh Bridge is a popular beauty spot; there are usually climbers tackling the famous Dewerstone Crags; and there is also a wealth of fascinating industrial archaeological remains.

The Dewerstone Crags

walk 15

START
Cadover Bridge

DISTANCE 3¾ miles (6km)

TIME 2 hours

PARKING Car park at Cadover Bridge

ROUTE FEATURES Steep, rocky descent towards Dewerstone Crags; uneven, narrow path through North Wood

GPS WAYPOINTS
- Start: SX 554 645
- Ⓐ SX 553 647
- Ⓑ SX 538 639
- Ⓒ SX 536 638
- Ⓓ SX 533 636
- Ⓔ SX 544 639

PUBLIC TRANSPORT None available

REFRESHMENTS Ice cream van in car parks; Royal Oak pub in Meavy; White Thorn Inn in Shaugh Prior

PUBLIC TOILETS None en route

PICNIC/PLAY AREA None

ORDNANCE SURVEY MAPS
Explorer OL28 (Dartmoor), Landranger 202 (Torbay & South Dartmoor)

Walk towards Cadover Bridge along the riverbank, and cross the river via the bridge. Walk a little way up the road, then turn left across the grass just before you reach a gritty track on the left. Aim for the granite cross that you will see ahead of you and slightly uphill.

Ⓐ Standing over 6½ft (2m) high, Cadover Cross sits on an ancient route linking Plympton and Tavistock. It was re-erected in 1873, but fell again and was restored by the Reverend Hugh Breton, vicar of Sheepstor, in 1915, and set in a large socket stone. Walk uphill away from the cross, keeping the granite wall on the left. Where the wall bears left, follow it round and walk along the open, grassy ridge of Wigford Down. There are Bronze Age hut circles and cairns in the area, dating from around 1000BC. Follow the line of the ridge past Oxen Tor; the path dips down and up again to reach Dewerstone Rock 745ft (227m), crossing a line of Iron Age fortifications on the way, with wonderful views of the Plym Valley to the left. Plymouth Sound is visible

> **?** *There is an inscription on the top of Dewerstone Rock. Can you make out the name of the person whose memorial this is?*

The Plym above Shaugh Bridge

from the top of the rock.

B Turn left from the rock and pick your way steeply downhill on a grassy path towards the wooded valley of the Plym. The path crosses a broken-down granite wall then falls steeply through oak woodland to reach the top of the Dewerstone Crags. Look for a path leading away right through the woods, and follow that path along the side of the hill. Where it meets a paved track, turn left **C** and zigzag down through the trees. The track here has been restored; this area, known as Goodameavy, is an SSSI and is in the care of the National Trust. At the end of the track cross the Plym just above Shaugh Bridge (late 1820s) on a gated wooden footbridge, then take the path (left) into the car park **D**. The Plym and Meavy rivers meet at this point.

* The **Dewerstone Crags** have many associations with the Devil, whose hounds are believed to round up unrepentant sinners and force them over the edge of the crags. It is also said that the woods here are haunted by an enormous evil red-eyed dog. The Devil is, not surprisingly, known locally as 'Dewer'.

Walk through the car park towards the road, noting the drying kilns on the left; from now on the walk is peppered with evidence of the old china clay industry. Before reaching the road turn left up steep stone steps and follow the path above the road, signed for Cadover Bridge. Look out for the remains of an old settling tank to the left of the path, just before crossing a wooden stile. The path runs steeply uphill (muddy in winter), then broadens and becomes more open, with good views to the right. Pass a footpath post on a field edge and keep uphill to another path junction by a stile (with a modern house to the right). Keep ahead as signed under trees; immediately the first piece of pipeline can be seen, half-buried under the surface of the path. Pass another settling tank on the left, after which the path levels and leads through light oak, ash, birch and rowan woodland. Across the Plym Valley to the left are great views of the Dewerstone Crags.

Follow the path over a stile **E** into North Wood (NT), still looking out for evidence of the pipe. This is beautiful oak woodland, with areas of soft green grass and the pretty, rocky River Plym below to the left; there are lots of good places for picnics and toe-dipping. Follow the path over a wooden footbridge and stile, across the corner of a field, then up a wooden ladder over a wall and back into woodland. Keep ahead on the lower of two paths. Eventually pass through a small willow plantation, through a gate and into the car park. ■

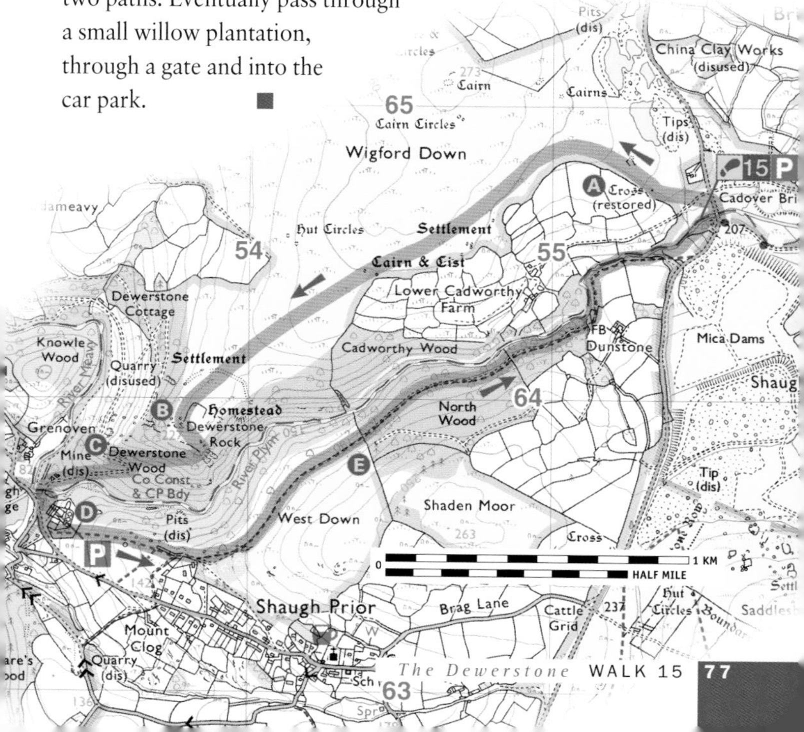

Wistman's Wood

- Ancient oak wood
- stepping stones
- Devonport Leat
- moorland views

walk 16

If you want to escape from any signs of civilisation within a few minutes of leaving your car, this is the walk for you. A rough track leads to Wistman's Wood, a magical ancient upland oak woodland, from where you set out across open moorland to cross the West Dart River on stepping stones, before an easy return along the banks of the Devonport Leat.

Wistman's Wood

walk 16

START Two Bridges Hotel

DISTANCE $4\frac{1}{2}$ miles (7.2km)

TIME $2\frac{1}{2}$ hours

PARKING Parking area opposite the Two Bridges Hotel just west of the B3212/3357 junction

ROUTE FEATURES Rough, open moorland beyond Wistman's Wood; river crossing at weir or on granite boulders; *do not attempt this walk after very heavy rainfall*

GPS WAYPOINTS

- Start SX 609 751
- A SX 610 757
- B SX 613 769
- C SX 609 780
- D SX 608 760
- E SX 603 753

PUBLIC TRANSPORT Bus service from Exeter, Plymouth and Tavistock

REFRESHMENTS Pubs and cafés in Princetown; cream teas in summer at Powder Mills; Two Bridges Hotel

PUBLIC TOILETS None en route

PICNIC/PLAY AREA None

ORDNANCE SURVEY MAPS Explorer OL28 (Dartmoor), Landranger 191 (Okehampton & North Dartmoor)

From the car park pass through the gate (signed Wistman's Wood) and follow the broad, stony track, which ends at Crockern Tor Farm; pass to the right of the farm over a rocky path to reach a footpath post **A**, and soon after the first view of Wistman's Wood ahead, nestling on the right bank of the West Dart River.

Follow the track on; a small path soon leads off right to Crockern Tor 1,312ft (400m). The track passes through a granite wall, then starts to descend – alongside various other paths – towards the wood. Look across the valley to spot the Devonport Leat. Cross a ladder-stile at the boundary of Crockern Tor and Longaford Newtakes, and go on across open grassy moorland to reach Wistman's Wood **B**. This

> * Equidistant from the stannary towns of Ashburton, Chagford, Plympton and Tavistock, and at the centre of Dartmoor's tin-mining areas, **Crockern Tor** is famous as the ancient site of the Great Court, the stannary parliament where tin-mining representatives met to regulate the industry. One natural rock formation does indeed resemble a giant chair, and is known as the Parliament Rock or Judge's Chair. The first records of the Great Court date from 1474, although meetings could have been held earlier. The last meeting (in Moretonhampstead) was held in 1786.

extraordinary and atmospheric place is said to be a favoured haunt of the Devil's hounds, which round up sinners and drive them into the dense woodland, from where they never escape.

Pick your way carefully along the top edge of the wood. The path is bouldery, and later runs uphill to meet a more obvious path heading north. Pass the last two or three clumps of oaks, and keep straight on; this part of the route is over uneven, open moorland. Look right to see Longaford Tor 1,663ft (507m), below which is the site of a mid-to-late 19th-century gunpowder factory. Walk on, keeping along the contours rather than dropping down to the river, where the land is boggy. Look ahead and left, towards the head weir of the leat on the opposite bank, and you will see a ladder-stile on this side of the river; aim for the stile.

> * **Wistman's Wood** (NNR) is one of only three remaining areas of ancient upland oak woodland on the moor, the others being Piles Copse, on the Erme, and Blackator Copse, on the West Okement River. It is an enchanting place: the twisted, stunted oaks, growing from a bed of moss-covered boulders (which have protected them from destructive grazing) are festooned with tree ferns and lichens, many of which can survive here because of the lack of air pollution.

C Cross the stile. You can cross the river at the weir (built in the 1790s) – at low water only – or turn left and cross it on large boulders about 50 yds (46m) down river, where a big flat rock juts out from the bank. Scramble up the opposite bank to find the 27-mile (43km) long Devonport Leat, an amazing feat of late 18th-century engineering *(for more details see Crazywell Pool, Walk 11)*. It provides a very attractive, level route high above the West Dart, enhanced by the combined sounds of its own tinkling waters and the rushing river below. Follow the narrow path along the left bank of the leat around the contours of Beardown Hill, crossing one stile en route, towards a coniferous plantation. Just before the woodland, climb around two small granite walls by a concrete bridge, and continue along the leat to enter the plantation over a stile D.

Follow the path along the

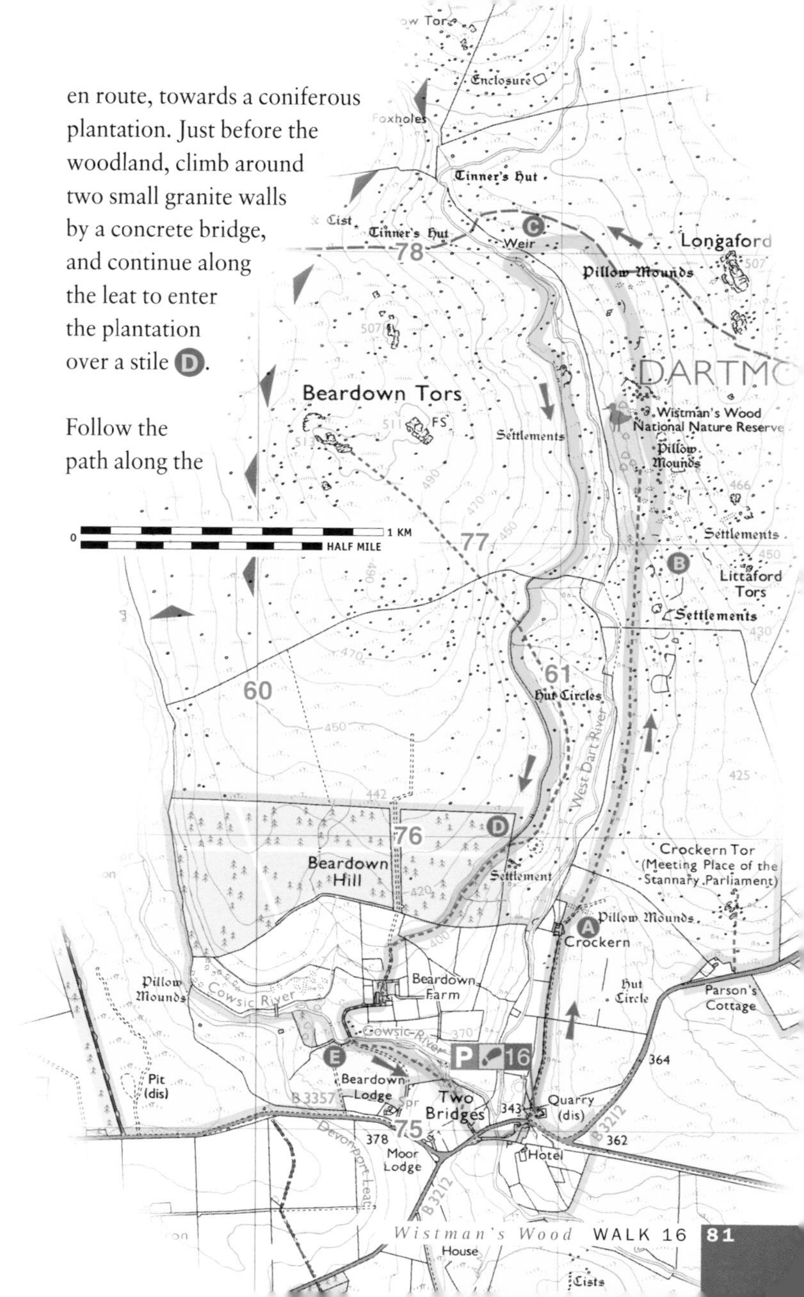

The path to Wistman's Wood

left bank through the dark conifers to emerge over a stile, then cross another stile, now surrounded by fields. Cross over another stile to reach a track. Turn left over a stile to leave the leat; walk downhill to reach the edge of Beardown Farm. At the farmyard follow the footpath sign right over a stile and down the track, with a line of beech trees on the left. The track joins another at a T-junction; turn right and drop downhill to cross the Cowsic River, following the footpath sign. Just over the bridge follow the sign left **E**, and clamber down steeply to walk along the right bank of the river. Cross another stile, and continue above the rushing river; then over a stile and along the bottom of a small field. Leave the field over a ladder up a granite bank, then a stile and footbridge, and across the next field. Over a stile, along a grassy track, and over a stile to gain the road just west of the Two Bridges Hotel.

? How many stone slab bridges can you count crossing the Devonport Leat?

Cross the road with care and turn left down the old lane over the second of the two bridges into the hotel car park; turn left and cross over the road to return to the car park. ■

Dr Blackall's Drive

- Granite tors
- wooded valleys
- scenic carriage drive
- ford

The views from this walk must be some of the loveliest and most wide-ranging on Dartmoor. The route follows a scenic carriageway above the deeply incised Dart Valley, then runs steeply uphill through woods and farmland to reach the tiny hamlets of Leusdon and Ponsworthy, before a final stretch across beautiful open moorland.

walk **17**

Cottages by the ford in Ponsworthy

walk 17

START Bel Tor Corner, north west of Poundsgate

DISTANCE 5¼ miles (8.4km)

TIME 2½ hours

PARKING Unsurfaced car park at Bel Tor Corner, on the Ashburton–Dartmeet road

ROUTE FEATURES Steep ascent up the lane from the River Dart and through Park Wood; also up the lane from Lower Town to Leusdon church

GPS WAYPOINTS

- SX 695 731
- Ⓐ SX 694 729
- Ⓑ SX 708 714
- Ⓒ SX 716 716
- Ⓓ SX 709 724
- Ⓔ SX 712 730
- Ⓕ SX 700 738
- Ⓖ SX 695 739

PUBLIC TRANSPORT Bus service from Tavistock and Totnes

REFRESHMENTS Mobile refreshments in the car park at times; picnic area by River Dart; the Tavistock Inn at Poundsgate (not en route)

PUBLIC TOILETS None en route

PICNIC/PLAY AREA None

ORDNANCE SURVEY MAPS Explorer OL28 (Dartmoor), Landrangers 191 (Okehampton & North Dartmoor) and 202 (Torbay & South Dartmoor)

Walk straight ahead from the car park (on the Two Moors Way), keeping the granite wall and Bel Tor on the left (inaccessible to the public). Sharp Tor 1,214ft (370m) lies ahead and to the right, just to the south west of which are the remains of Vaghill Warren, one of several sources of rabbit meat during Dartmoor's tin-mining boom. Venford Reservoir, built between 1901 and 1907 to supply water to Paignton, can be seen ahead across the valley of the Dart; the workers lived on site and were paid the princely sum of 12s (60p) a week, a good wage in those days.

Ⓐ The path turns left along a walled track; follow it as it bears left again just before Mel Tor 1,135ft (346m). Up until the 1950s a local custom was played out here. This involved rolling wagon wheels down the slopes of the tor to see if any could reach the river. The path drops down and bears left to run above the deeply wooded and very beautiful Dart Valley. This is the line of Dr Blackall's Drive, the views from which are glorious. Follow the level, grassy track, round Aish Tor. Just past a fenced-off quarry (right) bear right downhill on a broad grassy path, to reach a track. Turn left to reach a lane. Cross the lane and keep ahead to meet the road.

B Cross the road (small parking area) and follow the narrow path ahead to pass to the left of Leigh Tor. The path

*Scenic carriage drives were all the rage among wealthy landowners in the 19th century. During the 1870s, **Dr Joseph Blackall**, who lived at 17th-century Spitchwick Manor, had one laid out above the spectacular Dart Valley for his personal enjoyment. 'Dr Blackall's Drive' crosses the Poundsgate–Dartmeet road near the top of the hill above Spitchwick, and provides a very easy walking route today.

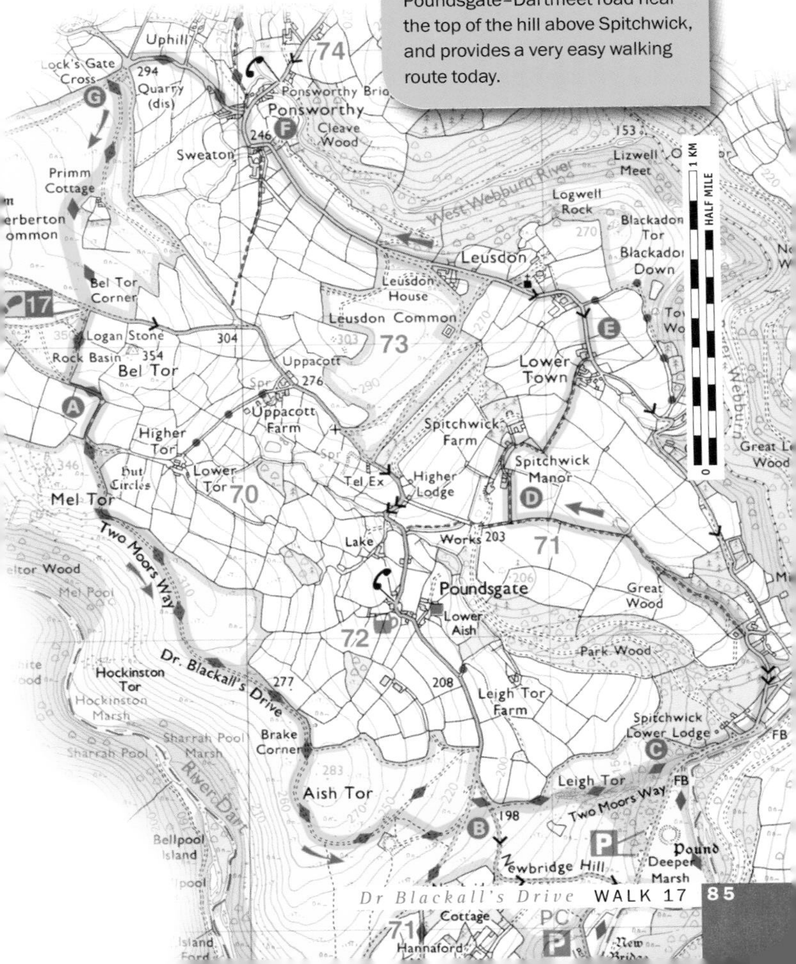

Looking towards Buckland from Leusdon church

continues downhill to meet the edge of Park Wood; turn right and drop downhill to meet the lane opposite the River Dart. (If you want to break for a picnic here, turn right to find a lovely grassy picnic area on the banks of the river.)

C Turn left to pass Spitchwick Lower Lodge on the left. Note the old metal suspension bridge (locked) over the river on the right. Just past that, turn left up a steep lane, signed Lowertown. Where the lane bends sharp right to cross a stream, turn left up a woodland track, signed Poundsgate. The track runs steeply up through Park Wood to a gate and stile at the top, to enter fields; follow the path, keeping the hedge on the right, to reach two five-bar gates by a pond (right). Go through the gate on the left and along the right edge of the next field, through a five-bar gate and another field, then through a gate onto a lane on a bend; Spitchwick Manor gardens are over the wall opposite.

D Turn right and follow the lane past Brick Cottage on the left. Just past the cottage turn right, following a path sign through a small wooden gate into a field. Keeping the hedge on the left, walk down the field to reach two gates. Go through the gate on the right and along the left edge of the next field; through another gate, along the next field and through a gate to reach Lower Town, part of the hamlet of Leusdon ('Leofwine's farm'). The narrow, gritty track joins the lane.

E Turn left to pass Town Farm and walk up the steep hill to find the church of St John the Baptist on the right, the building of which, in 1863, was funded by Charlotte Rosamund Larpent. A stained glass window in the west wall of the church commemorates her work, and the church replaced the Chapel of St Leonard, at Spitchwick. There are fantastic views towards Buckland Beacon and church from the churchyard. Walk on uphill; the lane levels off to pass a small lane on the left, and meets the tarmac road. Turn right and follow the road downhill into Ponsworthy.

* The tower of **St Peter's Church** at **Buckland** can be seen from Leusdon. The church clock is unusual in that, instead of numerals, it displays the words MY DEAR MOTHER, the creation of a local landowner who was also responsible for the carving of the Ten Commandments stone on top of Buckland Beacon 1,247ft (380m) in 1928. A second carved rock nearby commemorates the silver jubilee of King George V in 1935. The beacon originates from the time of the Spanish Armada.

F Turn left at Forder Bridge, where there is a small ford. Ponsworthy lies on a medieval packhorse route from Tavistock to Bovey Tracey, and the current Ponsworthy Bridge, which crosses the West Webburn River in the centre of the hamlet, bears the date 1666. The bridge is said to have been crossed by the Devil on a black horse during the great storm of Widecombe in 1638, on which day he also dropped in at the Tavistock Inn at Poundsgate, where the money he left in payment later mysteriously turned to leaves... Follow the lane steeply uphill; at the junction of lanes at the top (Lock's Gate Cross) go straight on, signed Dartmeet. After 50 yds (46m) turn left **G** on an unmarked grassy track (the Two Moors Way). Just before Primm Cottage bear right off the track to follow the paddock-edge bank (left). Bear left at the corner, then take one of two broad grassy paths bearing right uphill. At the hilltop cross the road into the car park. ■

? *On what date did Mrs Larpent, founder of Leusdon church, die, and how old was she?*

Fernworthy and Grey Wethers

- Ancient stone circles
- forest tracks
- remote moorland
- tranquil reservoir

walk **18**

A chance to experience the desolate wilds of deserted Teignhead Farm and the upper North Teign River, barely a mile from its source, and to visit the largest stone circles on the moor, via a wealth of attractive and varied woodland paths through Fernworthy Forest and around Fernworthy Reservoir.

Cattle in the valley of the North Teign River

walk 18

START
Fernworthy Reservoir

DISTANCE $5\frac{1}{2}$ miles (8.4km)

TIME $2\frac{1}{2}$ hours

PARKING Car park (charge) at Fernworthy Reservoir, signposted from Chagford

ROUTE FEATURES Rough indistinct track across open moor from forest edge to Grey Wethers; *dogs to be kept under close control around the reservoir (breeding birds)*

GPS WAYPOINTS
- Start: SX 669 839
- A SX 668 840
- B SX 660 837
- C SX 641 841
- D SX 639 831
- E SX 647 831
- F SX 652 834
- G SX 657 837

PUBLIC TRANSPORT None available

REFRESHMENTS Mobile café sometimes in car park; picnic area near car park; good range of pubs and cafés in Chagford

PUBLIC TOILETS In car park

PICNIC/PLAY AREA None

ORDNANCE SURVEY MAPS
Explorer OL28 (Dartmoor), Landranger 191 (Okehampton & North Dartmoor)

* In 1927 Torquay Corporation was authorised to extract water from the South Teign River, which now runs from the dam to join the North Teign at Leigh Bridge, near Chagford. The Teign (the name comes from the old dialect for river, 'ta') reaches the sea at Teignmouth. By 1929 a weir had been built, with an intake and pipeline running to **Trenchford Reservoir**; the Prince of Wales (the future King Edward VIII) visited the site in 1930.

Leave the car park with the toilets on the left; the information board supplies useful facts on wildflowers and wildlife. Bear left to pass through a bank onto a track and turn right. Look right towards the dam; increased demand for water for the growing population of Torbay led to Torquay Corporation being given authority to build a reservoir here, to dam the South Teign River, in 1934. Construction started in August 1936, and the 380-million gallon (1,729-litre) reservoir was opened in June 1942 at a cost of £246,000. There were originally three farms at Fernworthy, referred to as a 'village' in the 17th century, and in times of drought the old clapper bridge over the South Teign emerges from the bed of the reservoir.

Follow the gritty track towards the reservoir. At the next footpath post turn left **A** along a bark-chip path through the conifers, with good views of Thornworthy Tor 1,391ft (424m) across the water. This pretty path undulates through silver birch and rowan trees to reach another footpath post; go straight on (signed 'bird hide walks') to cross a double-railed footbridge and enter a grassy area. Bear right, then bear left at the next footpath post and walk up the grassy slope to pass a bird hide (with disabled access) on the right. Pass through the wooden gate to leave the Wildlife Protection Area. Walk straight on to join a track; turn right to reach the tarmac lane.

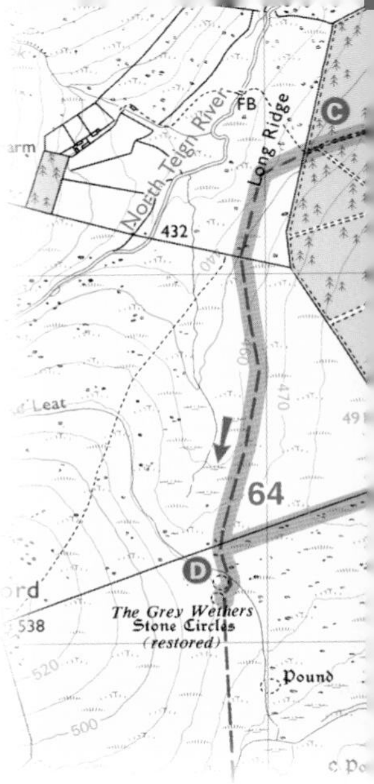

B Turn right; follow the lane as it curves around the south west tip of the reservoir and crosses a granite bridge. The lane ends at a small parking area. Turn left up a gritty track, signed 'to moor', which runs gradually uphill; at the next fork keep left. As the track drops downhill look right to see a small Bronze Age double stone row and stone circle in a clearing. Fernworthy Forest was planted from 1919 to 1936, originally to replenish timber supplies after the First World War, and then to enhance the scenic qualities of the reservoir. Fernworthy is Dartmoor's largest forest, covering almost 1,500 acres (680ha), and the swathes of Sitka spruce, Japanese larch and Douglas fir provide a wealth of walking and cycling opportunities. Keep on the track; at a crossroads go straight on to reach another crossroads of tracks at the hill top. Keep straight on; eventually the path levels off, then drops to cross another track and enter a dense conifer plantation.

C The edge of the forest is reached at a gate; ahead can be seen the ruined buildings of Teignhead Farm, occupied from 1808–1943.

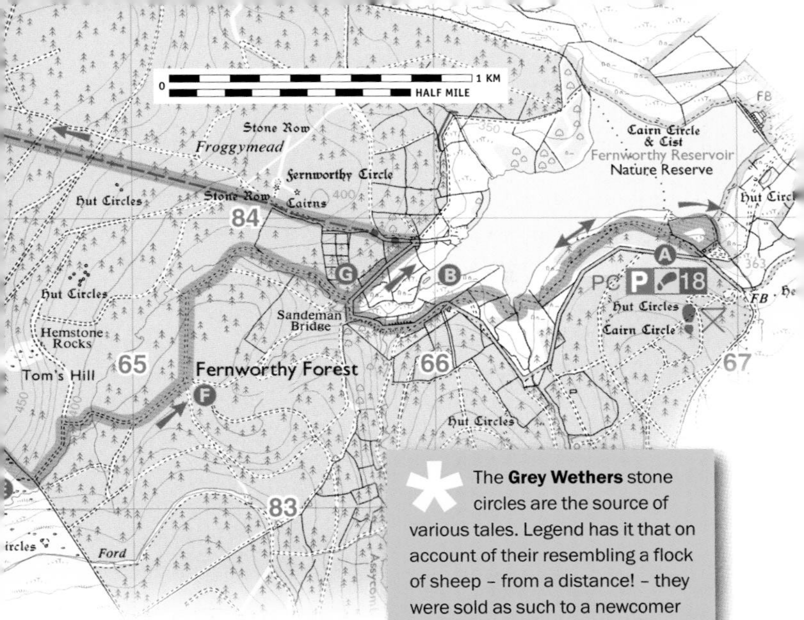

*The **Grey Wethers** stone circles are the source of various tales. Legend has it that on account of their resembling a flock of sheep – from a distance! – they were sold as such to a newcomer by a canny local; the deal was struck in the Warren House Inn. Another story relates how local unfaithful wives were forced to kneel in front of one of the stones; true repentance (or innocence) was rewarded by the stone remaining upright; guilt was proved by the stone falling on the unfortunate woman and crushing her to death.

Once through the gate, turn left to enter Teignhead Newtake and follow the rough path across the open moor, which runs about 30ft (10m) from the wall bordering the forest. Cross a broken-down granite wall; at this point the forest wall bears away left; keep straight on (parts of this path can be boggy). Look ahead to pick out a drystone wall which runs from Sittaford Tor 1,765 ft (538m) on the right along the skyline to reach the forest wall on the left. Pass through a gate in the wall and go straight ahead to reach Grey Wethers stone circles D.

These were partially restored around the turn of the century, by which time only about one third of the stones were still standing. In late Victorian times some people felt that the stones had been dressed – they are unusually rectangular – but they are all natural.

? Who lived and worked at Fernworthy for 50 years, and had a walk named after him?

Retrace your steps to the drystone wall, and turn right. At the forest edge turn right, and pick your way across tussocky moorland along the wall; the land drops steeply down to meet a spring in a small valley (boggy at times). Where the spring passes under the forest wall, turn left over an unmarked ladder-stile **E** to re-enter the forest.

Walk straight on along a gritty track, which soon meets another on a bend; turn right downhill. The track then leads slightly uphill; ignore the track coming in sharp right, and keep straight on to meet another gritty track on a bend, with a grassy track coming in from the right. Turn left **F**; the track runs downhill to cross the stream, then bends right to follow the stream back to the granite bridge crossed at the start of point **B**.

Grey Wethers

G Turn right on the lane to cross the bridge, then left on a track to leave the lane and pass through the gate by the bird hide. Retrace your steps back to the end of the woods; do not turn right up the track but keep straight on along the edge of the reservoir to have a better look at the dam. At times of low water hut circles are visible at the edge of the reservoir here. Turn right to walk through the picnic area and back to the car park. ■

Harford and the Erme Valley

- Waterfalls
- a Brunel viaduct
- wooded valley
- pretty hamlet

This walk explores a very quiet and unexpectedly lovely corner of Dartmoor. You are unlikely to stumble across the pretty little hamlet of Harford and the delightful valley of the Erme en route to anywhere else; and, once discovered, it is a secret you will probably want to keep to yourself.

walk **19**

Looking towards Butterdon Hill

walk 19

START Harford

DISTANCE 5 miles (8km)

TIME 2½ hours

PARKING By the church in Harford, signposted from Ivybridge

ROUTE FEATURES Riverside path wet and rocky in places; steep ascent up lane from railway viaduct to Pithill Farm

GPS WAYPOINTS
- (start) SX 638 594
- Ⓐ SX 631 597
- Ⓑ SX 629 591
- Ⓒ SX 630 589
- Ⓓ SX 635 569
- Ⓔ SX 633 578

PUBLIC TRANSPORT None available

REFRESHMENTS None en route; picnic tables by the Erme during point Ⓒ; pubs and cafés in Ivybridge; Cornwood Inn 2½ miles (4km) from Harford

PUBLIC TOILETS None en route

PICNIC/PLAY AREA None

ORDNANCE SURVEY MAPS Explorer OL28 (Dartmoor), Landranger 202 (Torbay & South Dartmoor)

Park by the church, on the lane leading to Harford Gate. Notice the little well in the wall opposite the lychgate. Walk back to Harford Cross and turn right, passing the church on the right. Follow the quiet lane downhill to cross Harford Bridge; there was a bridge here in the 16th century, and it is possible that part of the existing structure dates from the original. Follow the lane uphill under huge beech trees to reach the entrance to Hall Farm on the right.

Ⓐ Turn left through a wooden gate, following footpath signs for Ivybridge, and down the granite-walled green lane, with almost parkland-like-farmland to left and right. The swell of Butterdon Hill can be seen ahead and to the left. The track ends at a boggy area; pick your way across and through a gate into a field, with a granite wall on the left. Where the wall bears away left keep straight on uphill, aiming for a gap in the wooded bank ahead. At the gap, a path sign directs you straight ahead, keeping the coniferous plantation on the left.

Ⓑ A path sign directs you left through a gate; this runs downhill through woodland to pass through two gates and into an old oak wood, with splendid old granite walls, grassy glades and rowan trees. Leave this wood via a small wooden gate in a granite wall.

C Turn left, signed 'Ivybridge via Erme valley'. This narrow wooded path leads steeply downhill via two stiles to meet the River Erme, where you turn right to follow the river downstream. The source of the Erme lies seven miles (11.3km) north of Harford, in one of the remotest parts of the southern moor, near the sources of the Avon and Plym. The first part of the route along the river is unkempt and uneven; it passes over a railed wooden footbridge before tackling a couple of old granite walls and negotiating a very boggy stretch, but it is passable with care (and good boots). The next footpath sign directs you away from the river, then over a ladder-stile into a coniferous plantation. The path becomes easier, and the river speeds up to tumble through a series of narrow gorges, with waterfalls and deep

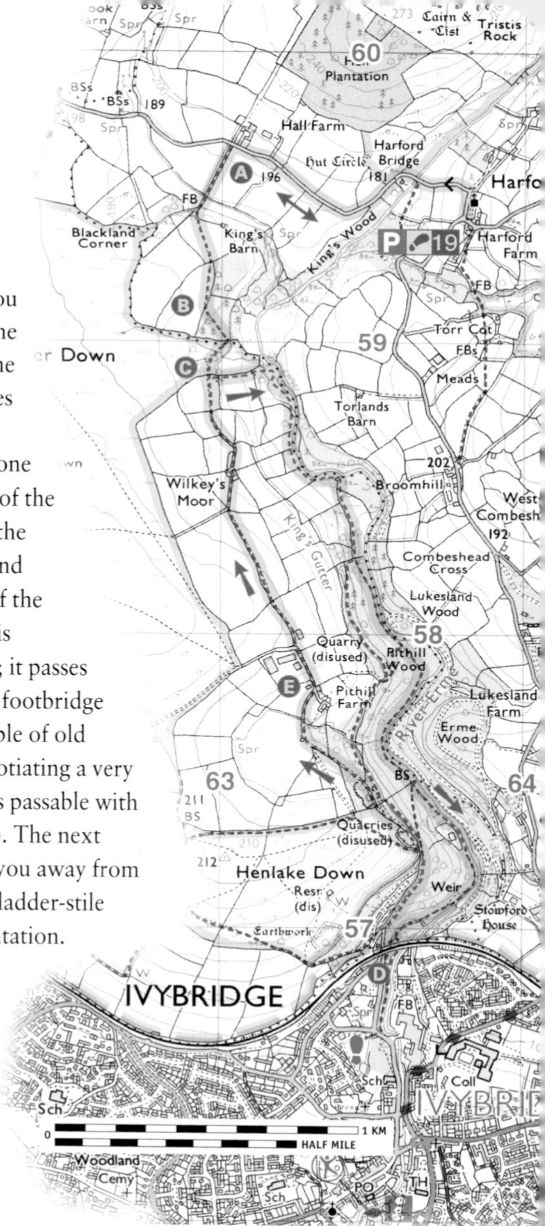

> ? *What will happen to you if you try to cross Harford Bridge in a vehicle that is more than 7ft (2.1m) wide?*

pools in deciduous woodland, complete with picnic tables. Follow the broad track on to pass a weir, then under the main Exeter–Penzance railway line viaduct to meet the road. The piers of the original viaduct (which had a wooden superstructure), built by Isambard Kingdom Brunel for the Great Western Railway, can be seen.

By Harford Bridge

D Turn right up the road to pass under the viaduct again. Ignore the lane left; where the road bends sharp left, keep straight ahead on the tarmac lane, signed 'public footpath Hall Farm'. The lane ascends steeply through woodland, but is very quiet. Where two footpaths lead off right into the valley, and another leads off left, keep on the lane, which leaves the woodland and levels off to end at a T-junction with Pithill Cottage and farm on the right. Turn left **E**; the next path sign directs you ahead through a metal gate and along a gritty track between high banks. At the top of the track there are two metal gates ahead; go

> * The **Two Moors Way** runs across Butterdon Hill. This 102-mile (163km) route runs from Ivybridge to Lynmouth on the north coast of Devon, linking the Dartmoor and Exmoor National Parks. It provides a wonderfully varied walking route, and joins up with a number of other trails, for example the South West Coast Path, the Tarka Trail, and the Dartmoor Way. It was opened on May 29, 1976. By linking with the Erme Valley and the Erme-Plym trails it is possible to walk from coast to coast across Devon.

through the gate on the right. A path sign directs you straight ahead along the track, with wonderful views of Butterdon Hill 1,204ft (367m) and Western Beacon 1,089ft (332m) – stone quarried from here was used to build the viaduct – to the right. The track leads to two metal gates; pass through, then along the left edge of a field, then several more gates (and cattle-grid) to reach the remote house at Wilkey's Moor; pass to the left of the house. Pass to the left of the barn, and ahead through a wooden gate to enter a lovely area of granite walls and oak trees. Pass through a gate and along the right edge of the next field, through a gap in the bank and straight across the next field, aiming for a wooden gate in the bank **C** (where the outward route drops down to the Erme).

* The upper reaches of the **Erme** hold one of the densest concentrations of **Bronze Age remains** on Dartmoor, including the longest stone row (possibly the longest in the world) which runs north–south for $2\frac{1}{4}$ miles (3.6km) and crosses the Erme and the Redlake. It was also a rich tin-mining area in medieval times; a good example of a tinner's hut can be seen on the west bank of the river about three miles (4.8km) north of Harford. These domed 'beehive' huts were made of granite, and used for storing tools and equipment.

Retrace your steps through the woodland, up through the coniferous plantation, and right across the fields to rejoin the walled track to Hall Farm. Once on the lane turn right and follow the lane back over Harford Bridge to your car. Have a good look at St Petrock's Church. There is evidence of a church here around the Norman Conquest, and definitely by 1262; the present building dates to the late 15th / early 16th centuries, and has a painted memorial to John Prideaux, a local man who became the Bishop of Worcester. The old granite cross by the lychgate was moved here in 1909, and was a waymarking cross, originally on the old route from Plympton to South Brent; the lane to the moor was known as 'the Brent road' in the 18th century. ■

Meldon Reservoir and Blackator Copse

- Highest tors
- ancient oak wood
- nature reserves
- moorland streams

walk 20

This is a walk for those who want to experience all that the high moor has to offer – but without going too far off the beaten track! The route passes within striking distance of Dartmoor's highest tors, and returns via a magical ancient woodland and remote river valley, giving the impression that you really are miles from anywhere: yet it lies within minutes of the A30.

Ponies at Blackator Copse

walk 20

START
Meldon Reservoir

DISTANCE 5 miles (8km)

TIME $2\frac{1}{2}$ hours

PARKING Car park at Meldon Reservoir, signposted from Okehampton

ROUTE FEATURES Rough approach over moor to Black Tor; rocky path through Blackator Copse

GPS WAYPOINTS
- Start SX 562 917
- A SX 564 915
- B SX 562 913
- C SX 568 913
- D SX 567 895
- E SX 563 894
- F SX 556 907

PUBLIC TRANSPORT None available

REFRESHMENTS None en route; range of pubs and cafés in Okehampton; picnic area by the reservoir

PUBLIC TOILETS In car park

PICNIC/PLAY AREA None

ORDNANCE SURVEY MAPS Explorer OL28 (Dartmoor), Landranger 191 (Okehampton & North Dartmoor)

Leave the car park via the steps next to the toilets, through the gate and turn left, signed 'bridlepath to the moor'. The tarmac way drops down to cross the reservoir dam via a metal gate. Look left here to see Meldon viaduct, now a scheduled ancient monument, built in 1874 when the London and South Western Railway line was extended to Lydford. It towers 150ft (45.75m) above the valley of the West Okement River, and is 541ft (165m) across. The dam was built between 1970–72 at a cost of £1.6 million, and is huge: 660ft (201m) long and 145ft (44.25m) high – an amazing 191 steps lead down into the valley of the West Okement below. The reservoir acts as a top-up supply for nearby Prewley Treatment Works.

* Two hundred years ago, the **Meldon** area was exploited for tin, copper, limestone, roadstone and aplite, arsenic, copper, granite and chert. Formerly owned by British Rail, the quarry covers an area of 235 acres (95ha), and produces ballast, roadstone, concrete aggregates and building stone. During the 19th century there was a copper mine near here on Black Down.

A Once over the dam, turn right and follow the broad, gritty track along the edge of the reservoir. Where a stile over the fence on the right leads to a waterside picnic area B, follow the track as it bears left and up the long, gradual ascent of Longstone Hill, with excellent views of the quarry and viaduct. You can still hear the A30 here, but as the track bears right around the end of the hill the only evident sign of civilisation is the line of red-and-white posts along Black Down, marking the edge of the military ranges. It is possible to walk within the ranges except on live firing days, but do not touch any military debris.

Just beyond the valley of the Red-a-ven Brook on the left the track (now grassy) splits C; keep to the left fork; at the next fork keep right. Dartmoor's highest points can be seen above left: Yes Tor 2,031ft (619m) and, just over the skyline, High Willhays 2,037ft (621m). The path becomes more patchy as Black Tor is approached, and crosses a boggy area on boulders; aim for the right-hand outcrop.

On reaching Black Tor D, turn left to gain the second and third outcrops, from where there are excellent views up the West Okement Valley into the remote heartland of Dartmoor. Retrace your steps to the first outcrop, drop over the edge of the hill and pick your way down into the valley. Blackator Copse covers the slopes below Black Tor. To get a proper feel of this enchanting place, turn left at the river E to enter the woodland. It is well worth walking to the far end – *the path is very rocky at times, and boggy at others,* but the experience should not be missed – and the banks of the West Okement provide an ideal picnic spot.

Retrace your steps back to E at the lower end of the copse. Note how barren the opposite bank is: the broad swell of Corn Ridge, rising to 1,762ft (537m), sweeps up and away from the river, devoid of vegetation and covered with clitter, caused by the erosive forces of freeze–thaw

> ? *In what year did Blackator Copse become a National Nature Reserve?*

on granite boulders. Follow the river downstream; the path is indistinct and occasionally boggy. Where a small enclosure around the river is reached, keep close to the wall; the land here is pretty wet. Just beyond the enclosure the path becomes more obvious, and passes a waterfall and a weir. The river runs through a deep valley, with pretty oak and rowan trees, to reach a level, marshy area known as Vellake Corner. Follow the narrow path which clings to the bottom of the slope on the right, eventually to find a small footbridge over a stream on the left F, but do not cross it.

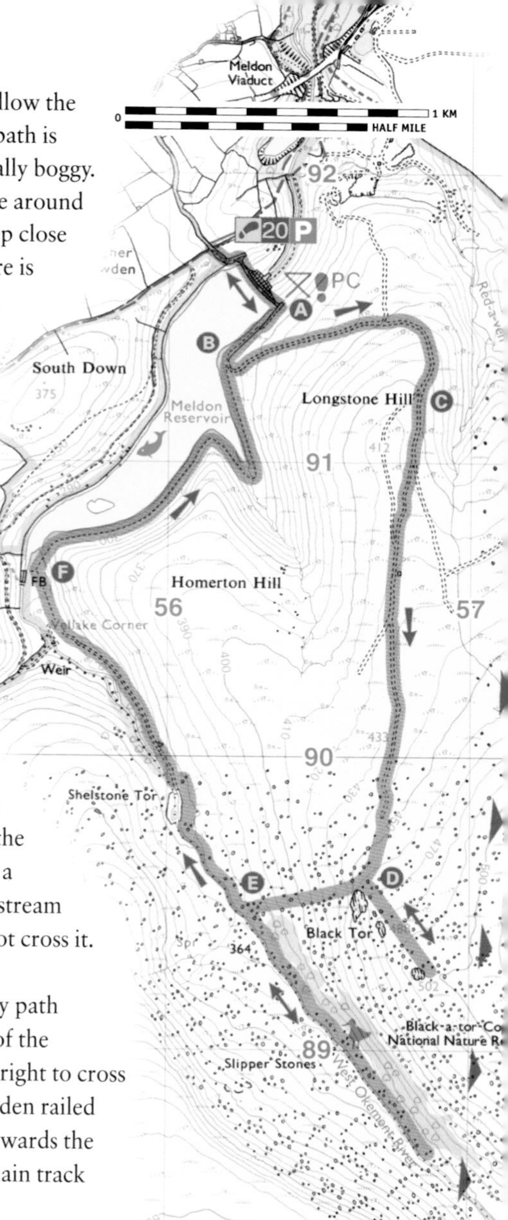

Follow the narrow, gritty path ahead around the edge of the reservoir; the path runs right to cross a small stream on a wooden railed footbridge, then back towards the reservoir to rejoin the main track where it starts to curve up Longstone Hill. Keep left, and retrace your steps back to the dam and your car. ■

* **Blackator Copse**, owned by the Duchy of Cornwall, is one of the best areas of ancient high altitude oak woodland in Britain and is established as a National Nature Reserve. **Wistman's Wood**, *(see Walk 16)* **Piles Copse** and **Blackator Copse** all share the same magical atmosphere.

Blackator Copse

Further Information

Walking Safety

Although the reasonably gentle countryside that is the subject of this book offers no real dangers to walkers at any time of the year, it is still advisable to take sensible precautions and follow certain well-tried guidelines.

View from Chagford churchyard

Always take with you both warm and waterproof clothing and sufficient food and drink. Wear suitable footwear such as strong walking boots or shoes that give a good grip over stony ground, on slippery slopes and in muddy conditions. Try to obtain a local weather forecast and bear it in mind before you start. Do not be

Sheep in the upper West Okement Valley

afraid to abandon your proposed route and return to your starting point in the event of a sudden and unexpected deterioration in the weather.

All the walks described in this book will be safe to do, given due care and respect, even during the winter. Indeed, a crisp, fine winter day often provides perfect walking conditions, with firm ground underfoot and a clarity unique to this time of the year.

The most difficult hazard likely to be encountered is mud, especially when walking along woodland and field paths, farm tracks and bridleways – the latter in particular can often get churned up by cyclists and horses. In summer, an additional difficulty may be narrow and overgrown paths, particularly along the edges of cultivated fields. Neither should constitute a major problem provided that the appropriate footwear is worn.

Global Positioning System (GPS)

What is GPS?

Global Positioning System, or GPS for short, is a fully-functional navigation system that uses a network of satellites to calculate positions, which are then transmitted to hand-held receivers. By measuring the time it takes a signal to reach the receiver, the distance from the satellite can be estimated. Repeat this with several satellites and the receiver can then triangulate its position, in effect telling the receiver exactly where you are, in any weather, day or night, anywhere on Earth.

GPS information, in the form of grid reference data, is increasingly being used in Pathfinder® guidebooks, and many readers find the

In the Erme Valley woodlands

positional accuracy GPS affords a reassurance, although its greatest benefit comes when you are walking in remote, open countryside or through forests.

GPS has become a vital global utility, indispensable for modern navigation on land, sea and air around the world, as well as an important tool for map-making and land surveying.

Aqueduct on the Devonport Leat

Follow the Country Code

- **Be safe – plan ahead and follow any signs**
- **Leave gates and property as you find them**
- **Protect plants and animals, and take your litter home**
- **Keep dogs under close control**
- **Consider other people**

(Natural England)

Useful Organisations

Campaign to Protect
Rural England
5-11 Lavington Street,
London, SE1 0NZ
Tel. 020 7981 2800
www.cpre.org.uk

Campaign for National Parks
5-11 Lavington Street,
London, SE1 0NZ
Tel. 020 7981 0890
www.cnp.org.uk

English Heritage
The Engine House, Fire Fly
Avenue, Swindon, SN2 2EH
Tel: 0370 333 1181
www.english-heritage.org.uk

Forestry Commission
South West England
Buller's Hill, Kennford,
Exeter, EX6 7XR
Tel. 0300 067 4960

National Trust
Membership and general enquiries
Tel. 0344 800 1895
www.nationaltrust.org.uk
Devon Office:
Killerton House, Broadclyst,
Exeter EX5 3LE
Tel. 01392 881691

Natural England
Level 9, Renslade House,
Bonhay Road, Exeter,
Devon, EX4 3AW
Tel. 0300 060 3900
www.gov.uk/government/
organisations/natural-england

Ordnance Survey
Tel. 03456 05 05 05 (Lo-call)
www.ordnancesurvey.co.uk

Public Transport:
For all public transport enquiries
in south west England:
www.travelinesw.com

Ramblers
2nd Floor, Camelford House,
87-90 Albert Embankment,
London SE1 7TW
Tel. 020 7339 8500
www.ramblers.org.uk

Royal Society for the Protection
of Birds (RSPB)
The Lodge, Sandy,
Beds SG19 2DL
Tel. 01767 680551
www.rspb.org.uk

Dartmoor National Park Authority
Parke, Bovey Tracey, Newton Abbot, Devon TQ13 9JQ
Tel: 01626 832093
www.dartmoor.gov.uk

DNPA information centres
High Moorland Visitor Centre, Princetown: 01822 890414
Haytor: 01364 661520
Postbridge: 01822 880272

South West England Tourist Information
www.visitsouthwest.co.uk

TICs
Ivybridge: 01752 897035
www.ivybridgewatermark.co.uk
Okehampton: 01837 53020
www.okehampton.devon-towns.co.uk
Tavistock: 01822 612938
www.visit-tavistock.co.uk

Community information centres
Ashburton: 01364 653426
www.ashburton.org/infocentre
Bovey Tracey: 01626 832047
www.boveytracey.gov.uk
Buckfastleigh: 01364 644522
www.buckfastleigh.gov.uk
Moretonhampstead: 01647 440043
www.moretonhampstead.com
Okehampton: 01837 52295
www.museumofdartmoorlife.org.uk
Tavistock: 01822 618539
www.visit-tavistock.co.uk

Youth Hostels Association
Trevelyan House,
Dimple Road, Matlock,
Derbyshire
DE4 3YH
Tel. 01629 592700
www.yha.org.uk

Ordnance Survey maps of Dartmoor

Explorer maps:	OL28 Dartmoor
	OL44 Torquay & Dawlish
	112 Launceston & Holsworthy
Landranger maps:	191 Okehampton & North Dartmoor
	202 Torbay & South Dartmoor

Answers to Questions

Walk 1: 1845.

Walk 2: They are rabbits or hares, a pre-Christian fertility symbol which links Chagford with ancient China.

Walk 3: Three.

Walk 4: At the house called 'Where the Woozle Wasn't' near Hayne Cross.

Pool at Swelltor quarry

Walk 5: 1881 D. Radford (who was responsible for piping a spring and providing three taps, so improving the village water supply).

Walk 6: 1893.

Walk 7: There are two: Drogo Weir and Fingle Weir (information board near car park entrance).

Walk 8: May 1929.

Walk 9: You are not allowed to swim; but you can go fly fishing (if you get a licence).

Walk 10: 20%.

Walk 11: From top to bottom: fox, deer, badger.

Walk 12: An otter; the name of the trail is attributed to North Devon author Henry Williamson's classic story *Tarka the Otter.*

Walk 13: They are corbels, cut in 1903 for work on London Bridge, but too short to be suitable.

Walk 14: Alfred James Hill (1889–1972), choirman, ringer and churchwarden, and John Clayton (1891–1973), parish treasurer.

Walk 15: Carrington, a local poet, who was born in Plymouth.

Walk 16: Four.

Walk 17: April 28, 1879 at the age of 85 (to be found on a plaque by the west window in Leusdon church).

Walk 18: Sydney Potter (details on board at start of Potter's Walk, to the right of the picnic area).

Walk 19: You will get stuck.

Walk 20: 1996; the answer is given on a noticeboard at the lower edge of the copse.

South West of England

Pathfinder Walks

1 SOUTH DEVON & DARTMOOR
5 CORNWALL
9 EXMOOR & THE QUANTOCKS
11 DORSET
21 SOMERSET, THE MENDIPS & WILTSHIRE
26 DARTMOOR
68 NORTH AND MID DEVON
69 SOUTH WEST ENGLAND COASTAL WALKS

Short Walks

8 DARTMOOR
9 CORNWALL
10 SOMERSET FROM BATH TO THE QUANTOCKS
19 DORSET
21 EXMOOR
28 WILTSHIRE FROM SALISBURY TO THE KENNET
29 SOUTH DEVON

South East of England

Pathfinder Walks

8 KENT
12 HAMPSHIRE, NEW FOREST & SOUTH DOWNS
25 THAMES VALLEY & CHILTERNS
37 LONDON'S PARKS & COUNTRYSIDE
54 HERTFORDSHIRE & BEDFORDSHIRE
65 SURREY
66 WEST SUSSEX & THE SOUTH DOWNS
67 SOUTH DOWNS NATIONAL PARK & EAST SUSSEX
72 COUNTRY WALKS NEAR LONDON

Short Walks

7 THE CHILTERNS
23 NEW FOREST NATIONAL PARK
24 SUSSEX & SOUTH DOWNS
27 ISLE OF WIGHT

Practical Guides

GPS FOR WALKERS
MAP READING SKILLS
THE COUNTRYSIDE COMPANION

For more information visit

www.pathfinderwalks.co.uk
tel: 01225 584 950
email: info@pathfinderwalks.co.uk
Twitter: @PathfinderWalks
Facebook: www.facebook.com/pathfinderwalks